D1716540

ISSUES THAT CONCERN YOU

Recycling

Viqi Wagner, *Book Editor*

GREENHAVEN PRESS
A part of Gale, Cengage Learning

GALE
CENGAGE Learning

Detroit • New York • San Francisco • New Haven, Conn • Waterville, Maine • London

Christine Nasso, *Publisher*
Elizabeth Des Chenes, *Managing Editor*

© 2009 Greenhaven Press, a part of Gale, Cengage Learning

Articles in Greenhaven Press anthologies are often edited for length to meet page requirements. In addition, original titles of these works are changed to clearly present the main thesis and to explicitly indicate the author's opinion. Every effort is made to ensure that Greenhaven Press accurately reflects the original intent of the authors. Every effort has been made to trace the owners of copyrighted material.

Cover image copyright Morgan Lane Photography, 2008. Used under license from Shutterstock.com.

LIBRARY OF CONGRESS CATALOGING-IN-PUBLICATION DATA

Recycling / Viqi Wagner, book editor.
    p. cm. — (Issues that concern you)
  Includes bibliographical references and index.
   ISBN 978-0-7377-4350-0 (hardcover)
  1. Refuse and refuse disposal—Social aspects. 2. Recycling (Waste, etc.)—Social aspects. I. Wagner, Viqi, 1953–
    HD4482.R43 2009
    363.72'82—dc22

                                                              2008046559

Printed in the United States of America
1 2 3 4 5 6 7 13 12 11 10 09

CONTENTS

Only forty years ago, recycling waste and discarded materials was considered a fringe practice of hard-core environmentalists. Today many scientists and others have concluded that recycling does have significant environmental benefits and social value, and the practice has gone mainstream. Today, says Neil Seldman of the Institute for Local Self-Reliance (ILSR), "more people recycle every day at home, school and work than vote regularly in elections." As an essential principle of the sustainability movement, which promotes development that meets present and future needs without depleting natural resources, recycling has become something of a buzzword. The new three Rs of the schoolroom are "reduce, reuse, recycle."

There's no question that recycling practices have reduced the percentage of waste going into landfills and incinerators in the United States. According to the federal Environmental Protection Agency, the percentage of discarded materials that are recycled rose from 5 percent (8 million tons) in 1968 to 32.5 percent (82 million tons) in 2006. The number of cities with curbside recycling programs has risen from a handful in 1970 (in those days even drop-off recycling centers were rare) to more than nine thousand today. Seldman cites eight reasons for this success, seven of which are relatively uncontroversial:

- [Legislation specifying] minimum recycled content of new products sold in a jurisdiction.
- Variable can rates (known as pay-as-you-throw, or PAYT), which charged households for garbage but nothing for recycling.
- Purchasing preferences that favored recycled-content products.
- Financial authorities that transferred funds through tax incentives, disposal surcharges, container deposits, and bonds from waste to recycling.

- Recycling industrial development zones that are reserved for recycling plants.
- Bans on disposing of yard debris, construction and demolition debris, and computers and other recyclable materials from landfills and incinerators.
- Bans on the use of problem products such as polystyrene food and drink containers.

The eighth reason, however, has been controversial from the beginning and remains one of the most polarizing issues in recycling:

- Mandatory recycling for households, businesses, and government offices.

Today thirty of the nation's one hundred largest cities have some form of mandatory recycling—defined as programs that require consumers by law to separate their trash so that recyclables are not dumped in landfills or incinerated, with penalties for noncompliance such as fines or refusal to pick up the trash. Thousands of smaller communities have established or are considering similar programs, despite vocal opposition. Is mandatory recycling a good way to get more people to recycle more waste? And even if it is effective, do governments have the right to force people to spend time and effort cleaning and sorting their own trash?

Support for Mandatory Recycling

Supporters say mandatory recycling is justified to address urgent environmental problems such as climate change. They argue that not only more metals, paper, and glass but also food and yard waste must be diverted from landfills, where it produces methane, one of the major greenhouse gases. This argument rests on moral grounds: Everyone shares responsibility for environmental pollution, resource depletion, and global warming, so everyone has a moral obligation to work toward solutions.

Besides, supporters maintain, waste diversion rates (combined recycling, composting, and source reduction) have plateaued at

In a recycling plant, a giant claw lifts recyclable materials for processing.

30 to 33 percent for years under mostly voluntary programs, proof that voluntary incentives have reached their limit. It's human nature, they say: There will always be people who respond to the carrot and people who only respond to the stick.

Case in point: Seattle's recycling success story. Before mandatory recycling began in January 2006, 38 percent of the city's waste stream was being diverted from landfills; since enforcement started, rates have exceeded 50 percent, and only 133 garbage cans have been left behind for violations out of 150,000 household cans collected each week. Another example: The village of Hamburg, New York, enacted a mandatory recycling program in 1981; the compliance level quickly exceeded 95 percent and has stayed that high ever since.

Popular support for mandatory recycling is high, advocates say. A November 2007 national poll commissioned by the founders of America Recycles Day reported that more than half of Americans support mandatory household recycling to help reduce global warming. In a recent Californians Against Waste poll, 97 percent of respondents favor mandatory recycling in large office buildings, and so-called Extended Producer Responsibility laws have become a very popular way to force manufacturers of computers and other electronic consumer goods to recycle electronic waste, or e-waste.

Opposition to Mandatory Recycling

Opponents of mandatory recycling are not buying these arguments. First, they counter, lots of places have achieved recycling rates much higher than 30 percent without mandatory recycling. Sixty-four percent of San Jose, California, households, for example, recycle their refuse through a voluntary city program.

Conversely, opponents contend that mandatory recycling is no guarantee that recycling rates will rise. As reporter Jim McCaffrey wrote in a 2006 *Evening Bulletin* article: "In 1987, when Philadelphia became the first major city in the country to pass a mandatory recycling law, the ordinance mandated a 50% recycling rate. The percentage was modifed in 1991 to a more realistic goal of 35% to 40%. The city has never approached that goal. The city never exceeded a 7% recycling rate."

Many people object to mandatory recycling on practical grounds, as an enforcement nightmare. First, it's confusing: There is no standardized system of tagging curbside bins to identify both unacceptable garbage in the recyclables and unacceptable recyclables in the garbage, and no standard definition of what must and must not be recycled. Second, it's unrealistic to expect trash collectors to examine and categorize the contents of every can, and impossible to keep dishonest consumers from tossing banned material in someone else's bins, which means endless disputes over penalties. Moreover, many communities have had to follow mandatory recycling ordinances with anti-scavenging ordinances to deter unauthorized people from picking up those curbside recyclables to sell to private scrap processors, which only adds more layers of enforcement bureaucracy and cost. Recycling is already more costly than landfilling, opponents argue; mandatory programs could break municipal budgets.

Critics also argue that PAYT and other positive incentives are more likely to change human behavior than punishment. Recycling rates in PAYT communities, they point out, average 17.1 percent versus 13.6 percent in non-PAYT communities. They urge first trying innovative approaches to increase voluntary compliance, such as RecycleBank, a program launched by Columbia University grad student Scott Kaufman in 2006. RecycleBank participants are given a recycling bin with a computer chip embedded in it. Garbage trucks retrofitted with a scale and scanner weigh and scan the bin on collection day, the information is recorded, and consumers are rewarded when certain weight thresholds are reached with "RecycleBank Dollars," which they can spend at partner businesses such as Starbucks and Home Depot.

Finally, many critics of mandatory recycling resent coercion on principle. As one San Francisco resident defiantly responded in 2008 to Mayor Gavin Newsom's ambitious mandatory recycling and composting legislation that would levy one-hundred-dollar fines for unsorted trash: "Do we want our garbage collectors to be the meter maids of trash? . . . I will stop recycling if this law goes into effect just to become an eventual test case. Dictators are anathema, no matter which side of the political spectrum they come from."

The contributors to this book examine the costs and benefits of recycling, both voluntary and mandatory, in the effort to reduce confusion about this complex issue and involve people in the difficult process of reducing the waste stream.

In addition, the volume includes a bibliography, a list of organizations to contact for further information, and other useful appendixes. The appendix titled "What You Should Know About Recycling" offers vital facts about recycling and how it affects young people. The appendix "What You Should Do About Recycling" discusses various solutions to the problem of waste disposal. These many useful features make *Issues That Concern You: Recycling* a valuable resource. Given the growing costs of waste disposal to society, having a greater understanding of the recycling issue is critical.

ONE

The Benefits of Recycling Outweigh the Costs

Economist

Published in London since 1843, the *Economist* is a weekly newspaper of international political and business analysis and opinion. Its articles, always unsigned, are written in plain language to "persuade the expert and reach the amateur." In the following viewpoint the *Economist* finds four major advantages of recycling municipal waste over burying or burning it: Recycling reduces waste volume, reduces greenhouse gases and pollution, conserves natural resources, and takes less energy than manufacturing goods from virgin raw materials. The author finds one major disadvantage—recycling is more expensive than other kinds of waste disposal—but argues that processing recyclables in developing countries, where labor is cheaper and demand for raw material is high, is helping to solve that problem. Regulating the offshore recycling industry to protect workers' health and the environment, and innovations such as sustainable packaging, are needed to reach ambitious goals of recycling 50 to 70 percent of municipal waste by 2020 in Europe and a zero-waste target set by firms such as Wal-Mart, Toyota, and Nike.

It is an awful lot of rubbish. Since 1960 the amount of municipal waste being collected in America has nearly tripled, reaching 245m tonnes in 2005. According to European Union statistics, the amount of municipal waste produced in western Europe increased by 23% between 1995 and 2003, to reach 577kg per person. (So much for the plan to reduce waste per person to 300kg by 2000.) As the volume of waste has increased, so have recycling efforts. In 1980 America recycled only 9.6% of its municipal rubbish; today the rate stands at 32%. A similar trend can be seen in Europe, where some countries, such as Austria and the Netherlands, now recycle 60% or more of their municipal waste. Britain's recycling rate, at 27%, is low, but it is improving fast, having nearly doubled in the past three years.

Calculating the Energy and Environmental Savings

Even so, when a city introduces a kerbside recycling programme, the sight of all those recycling lorries trundling around can raise doubts about whether the collection and transportation of waste materials requires more energy than it saves. "We are constantly being asked: Is recycling worth doing on environmental grounds?" says Julian Parfitt, principal analyst at Waste & Resources Action Programme (WRAP), a non-profit British company that encourages recycling and develops markets for recycled materials.

Studies that look at the entire life cycle of a particular material can shed light on this question in a particular case, but WRAP decided to take a broader look. It asked the Technical University of Denmark and the Danish Topic Centre on Waste to conduct a review of 55 life-cycle analyses, all of which were selected because of their rigorous methodology. The researchers then looked at more than 200 scenarios, comparing the impact of recycling with that of burying or burning particular types of waste material. They found that in 83% of all scenarios that included recycling, it was indeed better for the environment.

Based on this study, WRAP calculated that Britain's recycling efforts reduce its carbon-dioxide emissions by 10m–15m tonnes per year. That is equivalent to a 10% reduction in Britain's annual carbon-dioxide emissions from transport, or roughly equivalent to taking 3.5m cars off the roads. Similarly, America's Environmental Protection Agency estimates that recycling reduced the country's carbon emissions by 49m tonnes in 2005.

Recycling has many other benefits, too. It conserves natural resources. It also reduces the amount of waste that is buried or

Studies show that Britain's recycling efforts have reduced its annual carbon dioxide emissions by 10 percent.

Energy Savings per Ton Recycled (Million Btu)

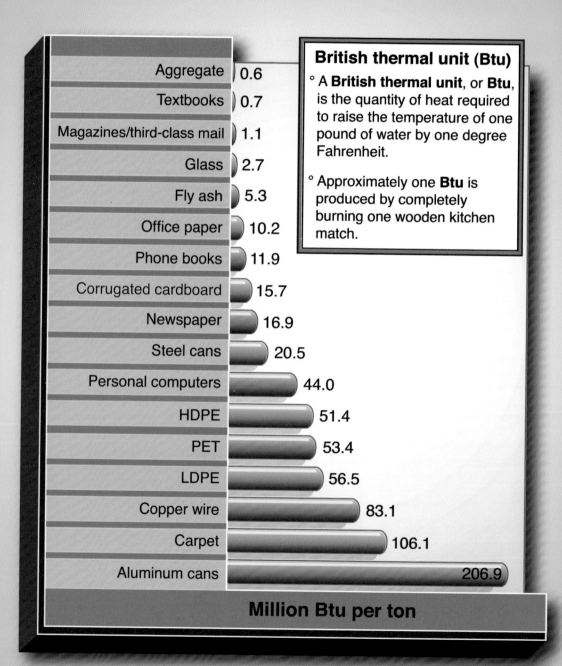

	Million Btu per ton
Aggregate	0.6
Textbooks	0.7
Magazines/third-class mail	1.1
Glass	2.7
Fly ash	5.3
Office paper	10.2
Phone books	11.9
Corrugated cardboard	15.7
Newspaper	16.9
Steel cans	20.5
Personal computers	44.0
HDPE	51.4
PET	53.4
LDPE	56.5
Copper wire	83.1
Carpet	106.1
Aluminum cans	206.9

British thermal unit (Btu)

° A **British thermal unit**, or **Btu**, is the quantity of heat required to raise the temperature of one pound of water by one degree Fahrenheit.

° Approximately one **Btu** is produced by completely burning one wooden kitchen match.

Taken from: Anne Choate et al., "Waste Management and Energy Savings: Benefits by the Numbers," ICF Consulting and the EnvIronmental Protection Agency, Washington, D.C., September 4, 2005.

burnt, hardly ideal ways to get rid of the stuff. (Landfills take up valuable space and emit methane, a potent greenhouse gas; and although incinerators are not as polluting as they once were, they still produce noxious emissions, so people dislike having them around.) But perhaps the most valuable benefit of recycling is the saving in energy and the reduction in greenhouse gases and pollution that result when scrap materials are substituted for virgin feedstock. "If you can use recycled materials, you don't have to mine ores, cut trees and drill for oil as much," says Jeffrey Morris of Sound Resource Management, a consulting firm based in Olympia, Washington.

Extracting metals from ore, in particular, is extremely energy-intensive. Recycling aluminium, for example, can reduce energy consumption by as much as 95%. Savings for other materials are lower but still substantial: about 70% for plastics, 60% for steel, 40% for paper and 30% for glass. Recycling also reduces emissions of pollutants that can cause smog, acid rain and the contamination of waterways.

Recycling Has a Centuries-Long Track Record

The virtue of recycling has been appreciated for centuries. For thousands of years metal items have been recycled by melting and reforming them into new weapons or tools. It is said that the broken pieces of the Colossus of Rhodes, a statue deemed one of the seven wonders of the ancient world, were recycled for scrap. During the industrial revolution, recyclers began to form businesses and later trade associations, dealing in the collection, trade and processing of metals and paper. America's Institute of Scrap Recycling Industries (ISRI), a trade association with more than 1,400 member companies, traces its roots back to one such organisation founded in 1913. In the 1930s many people survived the Great Depression by peddling scraps of metal, rags and other items. In those days reuse and recycling were often economic necessities. Recycling also played an important role during the second world war, when scrap metal was turned into weapons.

As industrial societies began to produce ever-growing quantities of garbage, recycling took on a new meaning. Rather than recycling materials for purely economic reasons, communities began to think about how to reduce the waste flow to landfills and incinerators. Around 1970 the environmental movement sparked the creation of America's first kerbside collection schemes, though it was another 20 years before such programmes really took off.

In 1991 Germany made history when it passed an ordinance shifting responsibility for the entire life cycle of packaging to producers. In response, the industry created Duales System Deutschland (DSD), a company that organises a separate waste-management system that exists alongside public rubbish-collection. By charging a licensing fee for its "green dot" trademark, DSD pays for the collection, sorting and recycling of packaging materials. Although the system turned out to be expensive, it has been highly influential. Many European countries later adopted their own recycling initiatives incorporating some degree of producer responsibility.

In 1987 a rubbish-laden barge cruised up and down America's East Coast looking for a place to unload, sparking a public discussion about waste management and serving as a catalyst for the country's growing recycling movement. By the early 1990s so many American cities had established recycling programmes that the resulting glut of materials caused the market price for kerbside recyclables to fall from around $50 per ton to about $30, says Dr Morris, who has been tracking prices for recyclables in the Pacific Northwest since the mid-1980s. As with all commodities, costs for recyclables fluctuate. But the average price for kerbside materials has since slowly increased to about $90 per ton.

Even so, most kerbside recycling programmes are not *financially* self-sustaining. The cost of collecting, transporting and sorting materials generally exceeds the revenues generated by selling the recyclables, and is also greater than the disposal costs. Exceptions do exist, says Dr Morris, largely near ports in dense urban areas that charge high fees for landfill disposal and enjoy good market conditions for the sale of recyclables. . . .

What Can Be Recycled?

For many materials the process of turning them back into useful raw materials is straightforward: metals are shredded into pieces, paper is reduced to pulp and glass is crushed into cullet. Metals and glass can be remelted almost indefinitely without any loss in quality, while paper can be recycled up to six times. (As it goes through the process, its fibres get shorter and the quality deteriorates.)

Plastics, which are made from fossil fuels, are somewhat different. Although they have many useful properties—they are flexible, lightweight and can be shaped into any form—there are many different types, most of which need to be processed separately. In 2005 less than 6% of the plastic from America's municipal waste stream was recovered. And of that small fraction, the only two types recycled in significant quantities were PET and HDPE. For PET, food-grade bottle-to-bottle recycling exists. But plastic is often "down-cycled" into other products such as plastic lumber (used in place of wood), drain pipes and carpet fibres, which tend to end up in landfills or incinerators at the end of their useful lives.

Even so, plastics are being used more and more, not just for packaging, but also in consumer goods such as cars, televisions and personal computers. Because such products are made of a variety of materials and can contain multiple types of plastic, metals (some of them toxic), and glass, they are especially difficult and expensive to dismantle and recycle.

Europe and Japan have initiated "take back" laws that require electronics manufacturers to recycle their products. But in America only a handful of states have passed such legislation. That has caused problems for companies that specialise in recycling plastics from complex waste streams and depend on take-back laws for getting the necessary feedstock. Michael Biddle, the boss of MBA Polymers, says the lack of such laws is one of the reasons why his company operates only a pilot plant in America and has its main facilities in China and Austria.

Much recyclable material can be processed locally, but ever more is being shipped to developing nations, especially China.

The country has a large appetite for raw materials and that includes scrap metals, waste paper and plastics, all of which can be cheaper than virgin materials. In most cases, these waste materials are recycled into consumer goods or packaging and returned to Europe and America via container ships. With its hunger for resources and the availability of cheap labour, China has become the largest importer of recyclable materials in the world.

Shipping Recyclables to Developing Countries Has Pros and Cons

But the practice of shipping recyclables to China is controversial. Especially in Britain, politicians have voiced the concern that some of those exports may end up in landfills. Many experts disagree. According to Pieter van Beukering, an economist who has studied the trade of waste paper to India and waste plastics to China: "as soon as somebody is paying for the material, you bet it will be recycled."

In fact, Dr van Beukering argues that by importing waste materials, recycling firms in developing countries are able to build larger factories and achieve economies of scale, recycling materials more efficiently and at lower environmental cost. He has witnessed as much in India, he says, where dozens of inefficient, polluting paper mills near Mumbai were transformed into a smaller number of far more productive and environmentally friendly factories within a few years.

Still, compared with Western countries, factories in developing nations may be less tightly regulated, and the recycling industry is no exception. China especially has been plagued by countless illegal-waste imports, many of which are processed by poor migrants in China's coastal regions. They dismantle and recycle anything from plastic to electronic waste without any protection for themselves or the environment. . . .

Far less controversial is the recycling of glass—except, that is, in places where there is no market for it. Britain, for example, is struggling with a mountain of green glass. It is the largest importer of wine in the world, bringing in more than 1 billion litres every year, much of it in green glass bottles. But with only a tiny wine industry of its own, there is little demand for the resulting glass. Instead what is needed is clear glass, which is turned into bottles for spirits, and often exported to other countries. As a result, says Andy Dawe, WRAP's glass-technology manager, Britain is in the "peculiar situation" of having more green glass than it has production capacity for.

Britain's bottle-makers already use as much recycled green glass as they can in their furnaces to produce new bottles. So some of the surplus glass is down-cycled into construction aggregates or sand for filtration systems. But WRAP's own analysis reveals that the energy savings for both appear to be "marginal or even disadvantageous". Working with industry, WRAP has started a new programme called GlassRite Wine, in an effort to right the imbalance. Instead of being bottled at source, some wine is now imported in 24,000-litre containers and then bottled in Britain. This may dismay some wine connoisseurs, but it solves two problems, says Mr Dawe: it reduces the amount of green glass that is imported and puts what is imported to good use. It can also cut shipping costs by up to 40%.

The Future of Recycling

This is an unusual case, however. More generally, one of the biggest barriers to more efficient recycling is that most products were not designed with recycling in mind. Remedying this problem may require a complete rethinking of industrial processes, says William McDonough, an architect and the co-author of a book published in 2002 called *Cradle to Cradle: Remaking the Way We Make Things*. Along with Michael Braungart, his fellow author and a chemist, he lays out a vision for establishing "closed-loop" cycles where there is no waste. Recycling should be taken into account at the design stage, they argue, and all materials should either be able to return to the soil safely or be recycled indefinitely. This may sound like wishful thinking, but Mr McDonough has a good pedigree. Over the years he has worked with companies including Ford and Google.

An outgrowth of *Cradle to Cradle* is the Sustainable Packaging Coalition, a non-profit working group that has developed guidelines that look beyond the traditional benchmarks of packaging design to emphasise the use of renewable, recycled and non-toxic source materials, among other things. Founded in 2003 with just nine members, the group now boasts nearly 100 members, including Target, Starbucks and Estée Lauder, some of which have already begun to change the design of their packaging.

Sustainable packaging not only benefits the environment but can also cut costs. [In 2006] Wal-Mart, the world's biggest retailer, announced that it wanted to reduce the amount of packaging it uses by 5% by 2013, which could save the company as much as $3.4 billion and reduce carbon-dioxide emissions by 667,000 tonnes. As well as trying to reduce the amount of packaging, Wal-Mart also wants to recycle more of it. [In 2005] the company began to use an unusual process, called the "sandwich bale", to collect waste material at its stores and distribution centres for recycling. It involves putting a layer of cardboard at the bottom of a rubbish compactor before filling it with waste material, and then putting another layer of cardboard on top. The compactor then produces a "sandwich" which is easier to handle and transport, says Jeff Ashby of Rocky Mountain Recycling, who invented the process for Wal-Mart. As well as avoiding disposal costs for materials it previously sent to landfill, the company now makes money by selling waste at market prices.

The Ultimate Goal: Zero Waste

Evidently there is plenty of scope for further innovation in recycling. New ideas and approaches will be needed, since many communities and organisations have set high targets for recycling. Europe's packaging directive requires member states to recycle 60% of their glass and paper, 50% of metals and 22.5% of plastic packaging by the end of 2008. [In 2007] the European Parliament voted to increase recycling rates by 2020 to 50% of municipal waste and 70% of industrial waste. Recycling rates can be boosted by charging households and businesses more if they produce more rubbish, and by reducing the frequency of rubbish collections while increasing that of recycling collections.

Meanwhile a number of cities and firms (including Wal-Mart, Toyota and Nike) have adopted zero-waste targets. This may be unrealistic but Matt Hale, director of the office of solid waste at America's Environmental Protection Agency, says it is a worthy goal and can help companies think about better ways to manage materials. It forces people to look at the entire life-cycle of a product, says Dr Hale, and ask questions: Can you reduce the amount of material to begin with? Can you design the product to make recycling easier?

If done right, there is no doubt that recycling saves energy and raw materials, and reduces pollution. But as well as trying to recycle more, it is also important to try to recycle better. As technologies and materials evolve, there is room for improvement and cause for optimism. In the end, says Ms [Kate] Krebs [executive director of America's National Recycling Coalition], "waste is really a design flaw."

TWO

The Costs of Recycling Outweigh the Benefits

Michael Munger

A simple test exists to determine if something is a recyclable resource or just garbage to dispose of at the lowest possible cost, claims professor of political science and economics Michael Munger in the following viewpoint: "If you have to pay someone to take the item away, or if other things made with that item cost more or have lower quality, then the item is garbage." By Munger's test, yard waste and glass are garbage and not worth the cost of recycling. Likewise, he argues, it makes no sense for either the cycling facility workers *or* homeowners to clean, sort, and recycle trash, because the end products are worth so much less than people's time, building and staffing recycling centers, and the resources wasted in making them. Michael Munger is chair of the political science department at Duke University and the author of *Analyzing Policy: Choices, Conflicts, and Practices*.

Near my own hometown in North Carolina, two recent news items caught my eye. The first was a statement by Greensboro councilman Tom Phillips:

Michael Munger, "Think Globally, Act Irrationally: Recycling," *Library of Economics and Liberty*, July 2, 2007. Reproduced by permission.

The net cost for recycling is more than double the cost for regular garbage collection that will go to the transfer station. (This is after selling the recyclables we can.) A lot of what we recycle winds up at the landfill anyway because of contamination or lack of markets for the recycled material. . . . While it "feels good" it is too expensive and we must look for better alternatives. (public comment, March 17, 2006)

This made me wonder: how could we *know* if recycling makes sense? What are the standards? Is Mr. Phillips right: should we look at costs?

The second was more remarkable, a parable of the costs of ignoring costs. It happened in Durham, home of Duke University. Here are the facts:

- Durham residents pay $60 per year for separate pick-up of "yard waste" (grass clippings, stumps, tree limbs, etc). Residents must separate the waste streams, putting yard waste in separate containers. Yard waste is "too valuable," as compost-in-training, to dump in the landfill.
- The city operated a facility that had become clogged with huge amounts of stumps and rotting vegetable matter. The $60 per year fee didn't come close to covering the extra costs of collection. No one offered to buy the "valuable" yard waste, for some reason.
- The stumps at the yard waste facility caught fire, deep in the huge pile. The fire could not be completely extinguished for weeks, and neighbors for miles downwind complained of the pollution. So the waste that homeowners paid extra for reusing was dumped instead in the main garbage staging facility.
- But the law prohibits disposal of yard waste in landfills in North Carolina.
- So, Durham shipped all its trash, including grass clippings, to a landfill more than 85 miles away, in Lawrenceville, VA.
- The clean-up and the extra hauling charges have already cost Durham an extra $1 million, compared to landfill disposal.

If You Have to Pay Someone to Take It Away, It's Garbage

The reaction of the citizens of Durham? We can catch a glimpse in this newspaper story:

> People such as Frank Hyman, a garden designer and former City Council member, *pay for yard waste collection with the understanding that the city is reusing it.*
>
> "That's my expectation, and I think that's the expectation of most people," he said.

Some experts say that recycling yard waste as compost is not cost effective for municipalities.

"A lot of people may be angry when they hear the city is shipping the yard waste to the landfill."

Reuse it? *For what?* The city is desperate to save money, and would surely use the stuff if they could. A question for Mr. Hyman: If yard waste is so useful, why do you have to pay the city to take it away?

There is a simple test for determining whether something is a resource (something valuable) or just garbage (something you want to dispose of at the lowest possible cost, including costs to the environment). If someone will pay you for the item, it's a resource. Or, if you can use the item to make something else people want, and do it at lower price or higher quality than you could without that item, then the item is also a resource. But if you have to pay someone to take the item away, or if other things made with that item cost more or have lower quality, then the item is garbage.

If yard waste were a resource, then trucks would drive up and down streets in your neighborhood, bidding up the price of your bagged grass clippings. That doesn't happen. *Ipso facto*, yard waste is garbage. No amount of wishful thinking, or worship of nature as a goddess, can change this basic calculus. Let's [apply this] to the problem of recycling glass bottles.

Clear as Glass: If Recycling Is Expensive, It Is Not a Resource

One of the most interesting treatments of the problem of markets and waste disposal is by an old friend of mine, Peter VanDoren. He writes:

Some policy analysts justify government intervention in refuse collection by invoking market-failure arguments in the collection of recyclables. Why don't free markets for recycling work? Well, in some circumstances they do. Scrap yards, for example, recycle iron and steel. The growth segment in the U.S. steel industry is the so-called "minimill" whose raw material is recycled. Recycling markets work fine in this sector of the economy because making steel from virgin iron and coal is more expensive than making it from recycled raw materials. In other areas of the economy involving glass, paper, and plastic, for example, the discrepancy between recycled and virgin prices often does not justify the development of markets for recycling. . . . [S]upport for recycling is more religious than economic in nature.

Markets can handle lots of things that look like "recycling." We reuse copper, even stripping it from old homes before they are torn down. I rent a car at Hervis, and take it back two days later so someone else can use it. And when I finish with the turkey at Thanksgiving, or the ham at Easter, I always boil the bones to make soup. That soup is much cheaper, and better, as a result of recycling the bones. None of these things is mandatory; we do them automatically, because they make economic sense.

What VanDoren means by "religious" is that the claims for recycling rest on an assumed, if not always articulated, moral imperative rather than on trade-offs or costs. But underlying this claim, for many people at least, is some murky idea that recycling "uses up" fewer resources than making things from scratch. Or, in the case of glass, making bottles from sand. As one earnest young staffer at a public works department in the northeast told me, "Recycling is cheaper, no matter how much it costs!" You can believe, if you want, that there is some mystical quality of products that make them valuable, and that price is the wrong measure of value. But if prices matter, lots of recycling we now do is irrational.

The difference between cullet (glass ground up by machines, using electricity) and sand (rocks ground up by nature) is clear: most cullet is full of additives, contaminants, and impurities. These contaminants are trapped in the cullet, inert and harmless. But if someone melts the cullet, an important step for making new glass, the contaminants can become toxic releases into the atmosphere, water, or soil. The impurities introduced by even small amounts of merged colors or types of glass in waste streams make mixed cullet nearly useless.

Sand, by contrast, is cheap and can be made into glass without extra steps, extra expense, or extra danger to the environment.

Recycling Uses More Resources and Energy than It Saves

So why do we recycle glass? Why is it against the law, in many cities and counties, to dispose of glass as garbage? *The fact that glass made from cullet is much more expensive than glass made from sand should be a hint that recycling uses more resources and more energy.*

Interestingly, in many cities, the answer to the "why recycle glass?" question is, "We don't!" Green glass, in particular, is so plentiful, and the cullet market so overwhelmed by excess supply, that disposal of green glass through recycling is prohibitively expensive. A number of cities have tried to delete green glass from the list of recyclable materials, but they face a political veto from recycling enthusiasts. And, interestingly, the political opposition comes precisely from those people who will end up paying more for the inefficiency of the recycling they insist they want. Taxpayers, citizens, the folks who take their garbage out to the street, want to ask the city to put green glass back on the recyclable list, regardless of the cost.

Incredibly, the pressures have been strong enough that some municipal systems have caved in, and either continued, or have restarted, accepting green glass. In a number of areas, private companies under contract with the city collect the green glass as recyclable, and then under direction from the city simply put the green glass back into the garbage waste stream. Given the resource costs of recycling, treating green glass as garbage is the environmentally responsible thing to do.

The Contamination Problem

Let me close this essay by focusing on "contaminants," another example of good intentions gone badly wrong. Two of the sources of contaminants in cullet that make it less valuable, or even useless, are (a) mixed types and colors of glass, and (b) food residues that remain on glass surfaces.

The first problem was discussed in a news story in 2006 in the *Arizona Republic*. Here's the interesting part:

> Nearly one-quarter of everything tossed into Phoenix's blue [recycling] barrels shouldn't be there. Removing all that non-recyclable trash costs the city nearly $1 million each year. . . .
>
> For residents who treat their recycling barrel like a garbage bin, the fact is sometimes lost that other people will eventually have to rummage through their cast-offs. "The question that I always ask children and adults alike is, '*Would you want to sort this stuff?*'" said Sheree Sepulveda, Chandler's environmental programs education coordinator. "It really puts a different perspective on it."

My mouth gaped when I read this. "Would you want to sort this stuff?" That's *exactly* what recycling zealots want us to do. Sort by color, sort by type, store separately, carry to facility and deal out your garbage in half a dozen little cubbyholes. It's as if time, our most precious resource, the one thing we can't make more of, has no value whatsoever.

Here's my perspective, which is rather different: does it make more sense for (a) a few workers, and specialized equipment, to separate waste streams, or for (b) all the rest of us, with far more valuable uses of our time, to spend time, gas, and effort separating "recyclable" materials and feeling good about ourselves by putting them in little separate slots in some expensive facility dedicated to this purpose?

Trick question! The answer is: *Neither*. It makes no sense for either the waste worker, or the homeowner, to separate waste streams, because the price system is telling us this is an inefficient and wasteful activity. If recycling were efficient, someone would pay you to do it. Disguising the costs by forcing citizens to do the labor, instead of paid government employees, changes nothing. It just reduces the explicit budget of the recycling program, and raises implicit taxes on the people.

Reasons for Not Recycling

"What is your main reason for not recycling?"

Base: those who do not recycle	Total %	Region			
		East %	Mid-west %	South %	West %
Not available in our area	15	13	10	20	7
It takes too much effort	12	26	10	12	8
It costs more to recycle where I live	12	5	10	14	12
I do not believe it makes an impact or difference	11	7	8	13	12
I am too busy	6	8	5	6	5
It is too difficult	5	6	9	2	9
No recycling center/drop off locations near	5	2	4	4	10
No pickup in area	4	8	4	5	3
Live in an apartment that does not provide separate bins	4	3	1	2	13
Don't know how/lack of information	2	–	6	1	*
Not mandatory	2	1	5	*	2
Other	6	8	5	8	5
Not sure	17	14	23	15	15

Note: Percentages may not add up to exactly 100% due to rounding.

Note: * = less than 0.5%

Taken from: HarrisInteractive, "One-Quarter of Americans Do Not Recycle in Their Own Home," *Harris Poll #67*, July 11, 2007.

And that brings us to the second type of contamination, food residues. Now, I have long heard of people running their mayonnaise or spaghetti sauce jars through the dishwasher before recycling them. But I had assumed this was an urban legend, since no rational person could justify the time and hot water needed to run garbage through the dishwasher.

To my surprise, it is actually easy to find examples of cities encouraging this lunacy. I found two examples very quickly, one from Beverly, MA, and one from Mason City, IL. But it is surprisingly common all over the U.S., in towns large and small.

"Recycle at All Costs": A Moral Bludgeon

Why would a city do this? Two reasons, and both of them are bad. The first we have already discussed: any costs imposed on citizens is avoided by city budgets strained by the irrational insistence on "recycle at all costs." Cleaner glass is worth more as cullet, and citizens' time and effort cost the city nothing.

The second reason is more disturbing. A generation of Americans has been indoctrinated into a "save resources, recycle at all costs" mindset. "Recycle!" is used as a moral bludgeon. This is different from "Don't Litter!" Littering is a collective action problem, a genuine social dilemma: cheaper for me to throw that cup out the window. But I myself would prefer a world where no one throws cups out of windows over a world where everyone does. "Don't litter" is an attempt to solve a real problem.

"Recycle, regardless of cost!" doesn't solve a problem; it creates one. Laws requiring recycling harm me, the environment, and everyone else. We have to take prices into account, because prices are telling us that we can't save resources by wasting resources.

THREE

Recycling Is Better for the Environment

Adam Beazley

In the following viewpoint "green design" advocate Adam Beazley argues for the environmental benefits of recycling paper, aluminum, and plastic. Besides conserving forests, mineral ore, and petroleum—the natural resources consumed in original manufacture—Beazley claims that recycling paper releases half the CO_2 emissions of virgin paper production, and every pound of recycled aluminum saves 7.5 kilowatt-hours of electricity and 4.5 pounds of bauxite ore from strip mining. The case for recycling plastics is weaker, Beazley concedes—plastic just gets made into secondary plastic products that cannot be recycled again and end up in landfills eventually—but recycling at least delays disposal, and people can still be environmentally responsible if they focus on reducing and reusing plastic. Adam Beazley holds a bachelor of arts degree in industrial design and science from the University of Louisiana at Lafayette. He founded the Web site Neutral Existence in 2007 to promote environmentally beneficial products and practices.

[I]s recycling] better for the environment or not? . . . YES, YES and Absolutely YES! I am not sure where people are getting these ideas that recycling is worse for the environment, but nothing could be further from the truth.

Adam Beazley, "Is Recycling Really Better for the Environment? Part 1: Paper; Part 2: Plastics; Part 3: Aluminum." *NeutralExistence.com*, December 13, 2007; December 22, 2007; April 9, 2008. Reproduced by permission.

Now, of course I can't just make that claim without presenting some sort of evidence to back up my claim. . . .

Part 1: Paper

Recycling Paper Is Better for the Environment

(*December 13, 2007*) When talking about recycling any type of material, a key term that will always show that recycling is better is source reduction. Source reduction is a direct result of recycling and affects the entire life cycle of the product. As it relates to paper, when you reduce the use of new paper, you are also

Almost twice as efficient as virgin paper, 100 percent recycled paper reduces CO_2 emissions by nearly half.

reducing the negative environmental effects of producing that new paper.

When a forest is cut down to produce paper, not only is pollution produced from the use of diesel machinery, but when the wood is turned into pulp, it releases all of the CO_2 that it has spent its entire life storing. Although trees are considered carbon neutral because they are only releasing the carbon that they have absorbed, the CO_2 released from the erosion of the topsoil is not carbon neutral because that topsoil loss would not have happened otherwise.

Now, let's first take a look at new paper production vs. recycled paper production using simple logic before we get into numbers and empirical data.

Virgin Paper	Vs.	Recycled Paper
Clear Cutting Loss of natural resources (trees) Erosion of topsoil Use of diesel machinery to cut and transport raw materials		**No Clear Cutting**
Paper Mill Wood releases stored CO_2 Energy to process trees into pulp		**Paper Mill** No new release of stored CO_2 Less energy to process paper into pulp
Consumerism Paper shipped to stores Paper bought, used, and discarded		**Consumerism** Paper shipped to stores Paper bought, used, and discarded
Paper to Landfill Paper is brought to landfill Paper biodegrades, producing methane		**Paper Recycled** Paper is picked up by diesel trucks and brought to paper mill

Now let's take a look at some actual CO_2 numbers:

Type Of Paper	CO_2 per lb.
Virgin paper 0% post-consumer recycled	7.14
33% post-consumer recycled	6.06
50% post-consumer recycled	5.50
66% post-consumer recycled	5.20
100% post-consumer recycled	3.90

The figures above have been taken from an extensive study done by the Environmental Defense Fund on paper production and publishing.

As you can see 100% recycled paper is almost twice as efficient as virgin paper and releases almost half of the CO_2 emissions as well. Now this is not even taking into consideration the loss of forests due to clear cutting and all of the environmental effects which happen as a result. . . .

Part 2: Plastics

Reduce and Reuse Plastics to Help the Environment

(*December 22, 2007*) Plastic molding is one of the most commonly used processes in product production. As a former industrial designer, I know plastics pretty well and because of the availability, cost and price per unit, plastics have dominated the product and packaging world. Unfortunately, plastics are terrible for the environment and recycling, although better than tossing in the garbage, does very little as applied to the plastic industry.

Unlike paper recycling, plastic recycling does not increase source reduction, in fact studies show that plastic use and plastic trash increase in areas that push plastic recycling. This is a little counterintuitive I know, but if you think about it, the reason for the increase is because of the increased positive perception of plastics as "eco friendly" because of the recycling programs. The danger of this type of thinking is that people buy and use more plastics, thinking that plastic is eco friendly because it can be recycled.

The simple fact is that most of the plastic that is placed in your recycling bin is used to make secondary products that are not recyclable, like plastic lumber, textiles and containers. Even though this is better than going to the landfill right away, it still does very little to reduce the need for virgin plastics, and the fact that the secondary products are not recyclable, the plastics end up in the landfills anyway, but just at a later time.

Unfortunately the virgin plastic manufacturers know all of this and realize that the increase in positive perception of plastics through public service ads focused on plastic recycling increases plastic sales. This [is] why the majority of all plastic recycling advertisements are bought and paid for by the virgin plastic manufacturers. Not only that, but plastic producers use the recycling logo (chasing arrows in a triangle) on every plastic item that is made, but the logo does not mean anything, the only important thing about that logo is the number in the middle which classifies the type of resin used in that item. The district attorneys in several different states are actually going after the plastic manufacturers for this false advertising and are trying to pass legislation to have the logo removed from non recycled plastic items.

With all of this being said, I still believe that it is better to throw that plastic item in the recycle bin rather than the trash bin, however, the main point of this article is to let you know the truth about plastics. The only way to truly help the environment where plastics are concerned is source reduction and the only way to do that is to be an environmentally conscious consumer. Here are a few things you can do to reduce your plastic usage:

1. Do not buy items packaged in plastic. Instead buy items packaged in cardboard or paper.
2. Only buy food items that are in glass containers. Instead of buying squeeze bottles of mayonnaise, mustard and ketchup, buy the glass containers.
3. Do not buy bottled water. Instead, invest in a good water filter, the result will be cleaner water and a better environment.
4. Reuse plastic containers. Plastic containers can be reused over 20 times before they need to be tossed in the recycling bin.
5. Use eco tableware for parties instead of plastic tableware. . . .

Part 3: Aluminum

Aluminum Recycling Is Dramatically Better

(*April 9, 2008*) Aluminum is 100% recyclable and re-enters the product stream in approximately 6 weeks. Unlike plastics, whose chemical bond weakens each time it is remelted, aluminum can be recycled an infinite number of times making it a true recycled material. So, by throwing your aluminum cans into the recycling bin, you are contributing to a process that conserves natural resources and saves money compared to manufacturing cans from virgin materials.

Recycling aluminum into new ingots to be used for manufacturing takes less than 5% of the energy it takes to manufacture aluminum from bauxite ore. It only requires melting down the recycled aluminum and removing impurities, which is much less energy intensive than mining bauxite and refining it into alumina to be used to create aluminum. In fact, for every pound of recycled aluminum the industry uses, it saves over 7.5 kilowatt-hours of electricity [and] it saves 4.5 pounds of bauxite ore from being strip-mined. To put it in human terms, by recycling one aluminum can you can save enough energy to light a 25 Watt CFL [compact fluorescent lamp] bulb for over 14 hours.

Currently Americans are recycling approximately 45% of all aluminum beverage cans and 36% of aluminum found in containers and packaging. Fortunately, the largest concentration of domestic aluminum use falls in these markets, so the individual has much more control over the end results than manufacturing industries. Unfortunately, the demand for recovered aluminum is shrinking because of an increased use of plastics in beverage bottles over other packaging applications. Hopefully the demand for recovered aluminum will increase again because of the new CAFE mpg [corporate average fuel economy miles per gallon] standards, which will require auto makers to use lighter materials to achieve higher efficiencies in their vehicles.

To answer the questions of whether recycling is better for the environment when it comes to aluminum, the answer is absolutely

The Aluminum Loop

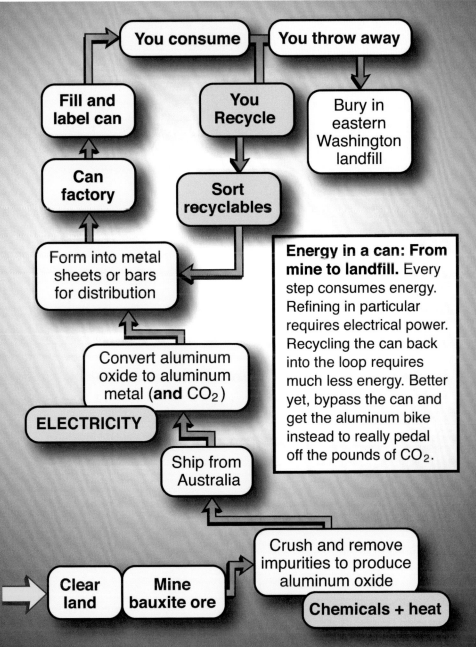

Energy in a can: From mine to landfill. Every step consumes energy. Refining in particular requires electrical power. Recycling the can back into the loop requires much less energy. Better yet, bypass the can and get the aluminum bike instead to really pedal off the pounds of CO_2.

Taken from: Doug Stark, "Does Recycling Save Energy?" *Re-Sources for Sustainable Communities*, Whatcom County, Washington.

yes. However, it does not stop there, if you really want to make a difference, try to NOT buy plastic beverage containers and opt for the aluminum containers instead and then recycle the aluminum container. This will not only reduce the use of virgin aluminum, but it will reduce the use of oil that is used to produce the plastic container which ultimately ends up in a landfill regardless of whether or not you recycle it. Remember, aluminum is 100% recyclable and can be continually recycled an infinite number of times and plastic is not and will generally be recycled 1 or 2 times before it is discarded.

FOUR

Electronic Waste Is a Major Recycling Problem

Elizabeth Grossman

In 2006 the International Association of Electronics Recyclers reported that 400 million consumer electronics—computers, televisions, cell phones, and other devices—are scrapped each year, only about 12 percent of which are recycled. According to environmental journalist Elizabeth Grossman in the following viewpoint, most of the rest of the world's so-called e-waste is stockpiled, dumped in landfills where its component pollutants and heavy metals contaminate soils and groundwater, or, increasingly, shipped to scrap processors in developing countries in Asia and Africa. There mostly poor workers in dangerous sweatshops are exposed to a "stew of toxic materials" that cause disease and litter the landscape. Elizabeth Grossman is the author of *High Tech Trash: Digital Devices, Hidden Toxics, and Human Health.*

A parade of trucks piled with worn-out computers and electronic equipment pulls away from container ships docked at the port of Taizhou in the Zhejiang Province of southeastern China. A short distance inland, the trucks dump their loads in what looks like an enormous parking lot. Pools of dark oily liquid

Elizabeth Grossman, "Where Computers Go to Die—and Kill," *Salon*, April 10, 2006. This article first appeared in *Salon*, at www.salon.com. An online version remains in the *Salon* archives. Reprinted with permission.

seep from under the mounds of junked machinery. The equipment comes mostly from the United States, Europe and Japan.

Fifty Percent of Electronic Waste Is Dumped in Developing Countries

For years, developed countries have been exporting tons of electronic waste to China for inexpensive, labor-intensive recycling and disposal. Since 2000, it's been illegal to import electronic waste into China for this kind of environmentally unsound recycling. But tons of debris are smuggled in with legitimate imports, corruption is common among local officials, and China's appetite for scrap is so enormous that the shipments just keep on coming.

In Taizhou's outdoor workshops, people bang apart the computers and toss bits of metal into brick furnaces that look like chimneys. Split open, the electronics release a stew of toxic materials—among them beryllium, cadmium, lead, mercury and flame retardants—that can accumulate in human blood and disrupt the body's hormonal balance. Exposed to heat or allowed to degrade, electronics' plastics can break down into organic pollutants that cause a host of health problems, including cancer. Wearing no protective clothing, workers roast circuit boards in big, uncovered woklike pans to melt plastics and collect valuable metals. Other workers sluice open basins of acid over semiconductors to remove their gold, tossing the waste into nearby streams. Typical wages for this work are about $2 to $4 a day.

Jim Puckett, director of Basel Action Network, an environmental advocacy organization that tracks hazardous waste, filmed these Dickensian scenes in 2004. "The volume of junk was amazing," he says. "It was arriving 24 hours a day and there was so much scrap that one truck was loaded every two minutes." Nothing has changed in two years. "China is still getting the stuff," Puckett tells me in March 2006. In fact, he says, the trend in China now is "to push the ugly stuff out of sight into the rural areas."

The conditions in Taizhou are particularly distressing to Puckett because they underscore what he sees as a persistent failure by the U.S. federal government to stop the dumping of millions of used

How Much of Our E-Waste Is Exported Each Year?

Each year we export more than 5,000 shipping containers of e-waste, which, if stacked in one column, would be over eight miles high—higher than most airplanes fly.

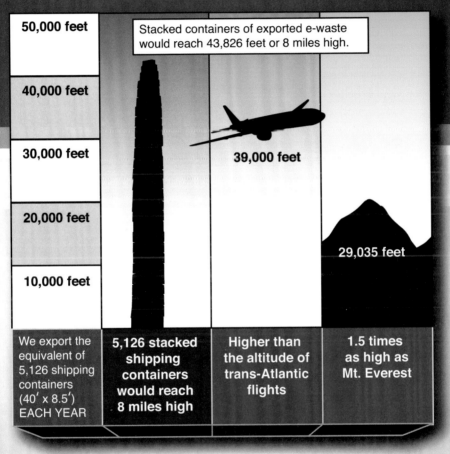

50,000 feet	Stacked containers of exported e-waste would reach 43,826 feet or 8 miles high.		
40,000 feet			
30,000 feet		39,000 feet	
20,000 feet			
			29,035 feet
10,000 feet			
We export the equivalent of 5,126 shipping containers (40′ x 8.5′) EACH YEAR	5,126 stacked shipping containers would reach 8 miles high	Higher than the altitude of trans-Atlantic flights	1.5 times as high as Mt. Everest

The EPA [Environmental Protection Agency] reports that only 12.5 percent of discarded electronic waste is recovered for recycling. That was 330,000 tons of e-waste in 2005.[1] But recycling industry experts estimate that of that 12.5 percent, from 50 percent to 80 percent is exported overseas. So if we use the lower 50 percent number, or 165,000 tons, that would fill 5,126 shipping containers, assuming 40-foot by 8.5-foot containers, holding 32 tons each. If you stacked 5,126 shipping containers in a tower, it would reach over 8 miles high, as high as 30 Empire State Buildings and 1.5 Mt. Everests.

[1] U.S. EPA, *Municipal Solid Waste in the United States, 2005 Facts and Figures*, October 2006. www.epa.gov/msw/pubs/mswchar05.pdf.

Taken from: Electronics Take-Back Coalition, "How Much of Our E-Waste Is Exported Each Year?" from EPA, *Municipal Solid Waste in the United States: 2005 Facts and Figures*, October 2006.

computers, TVs, cellphones and other electronics in the world's developing regions, including those in China, India, Malaysia, the Philippines, Vietnam, Eastern Europe and Africa.

Because high-tech electronics contain hundreds of materials packed into small spaces, they are difficult and expensive to recycle. Eager to minimize costs and maximize profits, many recyclers ship large quantities of used electronics to countries where labor is cheap and environmental regulations lax. U.S. recyclers and watchdog groups like Basel Action Network [BAN] estimate that 50 percent or more of the United States' used computers, cellphones and TVs sent to recyclers are shipped overseas for recycling to places like Taizhou or Lagos, Nigeria, as permitted by federal law. But much of this obsolete equipment ends up as toxic waste, with hazardous components exposed, burned or allowed to degrade in landfills.

Unsafe Recycling Practices' Appalling Toll

BAN first called widespread attention to the problem in 2002, when it released "Exporting Harm," a documentary that revealed the appalling damage caused by electronic waste in China. In the southern Chinese village of Guiyu, many of the workers who dismantle high-tech electronics live only steps from their jobs. Their children wander over piles of burnt wires and splash in puddles by the banks of rivers that have become dumping grounds for discarded computer parts. The pollution has been so severe that Guiyu's water supply has been undrinkable since the mid-'90s. Water samples taken in 2005 found levels of lead and other metals 400 to 600 times what international standards consider safe.

In the summer of 2005, Puckett investigated Lagos, another port bursting with what he calls the "effluent of the affluent." "It appears that about 500 loads of computer equipment are arriving in Lagos each month," he says. Ostensibly sent for resale in Nigeria's rapidly growing market for high-tech electronics, as much as 75 percent of the incoming equipment is unusable, Puckett discovered. As a result, huge quantities are simply dumped.

Photographs taken by BAN in Lagos show scrapped electronics lying in wetlands, along roadsides, being examined by curious children and burning in uncontained landfills. Seared, broken monitors and CPUs [computer processors] are nestled in weeds, serving as perches for lizards, chickens and goats. One mound of computer junk towers at least 6 feet high. Pucker found identification tags showing that some of the junked equipment originally belonged to the U.S. Army Corps of Engineers, the Illinois Department of Human Services, the Kansas Department of Aging, the State of Massachusetts, the Michigan Department of Natural Resources, the City of Houston, school districts, hospitals, banks and numerous businesses, including IBM and Intel.

Under the Basel Convention, an international agreement designed to curtail trade in hazardous waste, none of this dumping should be happening. Leaded CRT [computer monitor] glass, mercury switches, parts containing heavy metals, and other elements of computer scrap are considered hazardous waste under Basel and cannot be exported for disposal. Electronics can be exported for reuse, repair and—under certain conditions—recycling, creating a gray area into which millions of tons of obsolete electronics have fallen.

U.S. Inaction

The U.S. is the only industrialized nation not to have ratified the Basel Convention, which would prevent it from trading in hazardous waste. The U.S. also has no federal laws that prohibit the export of toxic e-waste, nor has the U.S. signed the Basel Ban, a 1995 amendment to the convention that prohibits export of hazardous waste from Organization of Economic Cooperation and Development [OECD] member countries to non-OECD countries—essentially from wealthy to poorer nations. While this policy is intended to spur reuse and recycling, it also makes it difficult to curtail the kind of shipments BAN found in Lagos.

Despite a growing awareness of e-waste's hazards, the U.S. government, says Puckett, has done nothing in the past several years to stem the flow of e-trash. Given the [George W.] Bush administration's reluctance to enact or support regulations that interfere with what it considers free trade and the difficulty of monitoring e-waste exports, the shipments continue. "Follow the material, and you'll find the vast majority of e-waste is still going overseas," says Robert Houghton, president of Redemtech Inc., a company that handles electronics recycling for a number of Fortune 500 companies, including Kaiser Permanente. As Puckett says, "Exploiting low-wage countries as a dumping ground is winning the day."

Dismantling and Processing Electronics Is Difficult and Expensive

Over a billion computers are now in use worldwide—over 200 million in the United States, which has the world's highest per capita concentration of PCs. The average life span of an American computer is about three to five years and some 30 million become obsolete here each year. According to the International Association of Electronics Recyclers, approximately 3 billion pieces of consumer electronics will be scrapped by 2010. Overall, high-tech electronics are the fastest-growing part of the municipal waste stream both in the U.S. and Europe.

The EPA [Environmental Protection Agency] estimates that only about 10 percent of all obsolete consumer electronics are recycled. The rest are stored somewhere, passed on to second users, or simply tossed in the trash. The EPA's most recent estimate is that over 2 million tons of e-waste end up in U.S. landfills each year. As Jim Fisher of *Salon* reported in 2000, a toxic stew from discarded computers leaches into groundwater surrounding landfills.

Current design, particularly of equipment now entering the waste stream, makes separating electronics' dozens of materials labor-intensive. "Almost every piece of equipment is different," says Greg Sampson of Earth Protection Services, a national electronics recycler. The process almost always involves manual labor and, once the electronics are dismantled, sophisticated machinery is required to safely separate and process metals and plastics.

The fragile CRTs with leaded glass used in traditional desktop monitors and TV screens pose a particular recycling challenge. Metals are the easiest materials to recycle and the most valuable—circuit boards typically contain gold, silver and other precious metals. Plastics are the peskiest, as many different kinds may be used in a single piece of equipment and markets for recycled plastics are far less established than those for scrap metals.

E-Scrap News, a recycling industry trade magazine, features about 950 e-scrap processors in its North American database—a list that doesn't include nonprofits or reuse organizations. And not all electronics recyclers offer the same services. Some dismantle the equipment and recover materials themselves. But many simply collect equipment and do initial disassembly, then contract with others for materials recovery.

According to the International Association of Electronics Recyclers, this business now generates about $700 million annually in the U.S. and is increasing steadily. Most recyclers charge fees to process equipment. But essentially profits come from the sale of materials recovered or by selling equipment or components to those who will do so. There's also a speculative aspect to the business, especially when the scrap metal market is booming and the value of recyclable circuit boards increasing—it reached an all-time high in January 2006 at $5,640 a ton.

Industry and Government Inaction as Illegal Waste Shipments Rise

Some recyclers—mostly smaller shops—acquire used equipment at surplus property auctions, on eBay or other such resale outlets, then resell equipment whole or in parts by the pound to what Houghton calls "materials brokers" and "chop shops." One batch of equipment may end up being sold to a series of brokers before it reaches a materials processor, and much of what these brokers deal in ends up overseas where costs are lowest. "If a company is buying your electronic scrap or untested equipment," rather than charging for this service, "it's highly likely that it's going overseas," says Sarah Westervelt of BAN. . . .

Currently, there is no consistent, industrywide or government program to certify or license electronics recyclers. As a result,

Old computer components pile up at an e-waste recycling center in India. The United States exports nearly 80 percent of its e-waste to Pakistan, India, and China.

says Houghton, "It's extremely difficult to peel back the onion far enough to find out where the equipment goes. It may change hands two, three or four times before it leaves the country." And, he explains, "The cost of shipping a 40-foot container full of computers, relative to the value of the equipment," even at scrap prices, "is pretty low." With dealers from China to Eastern Europe and Africa ready to buy used electronics for scrap or reuse, and U.S. domestic transportation and recycling costs high, it's actually more profitable to load up a container and send it to Nigeria or Taizhou than it is to process equipment at home.

So traveling the seas in the shadows of legitimate high-tech exports are huge containers that may hold as many as 1,000 used computers. They're loaded on ships at East Coast and Gulf Coast ports in the U.S. for Atlantic crossings, or at European ports, including Felixstowe, Le Havre and Rotterdam, arriving in West Africa by way of Spain. Others cross the Mediterranean from Israel and Dubai, or travel Asian Pacific routes from the U.S., Japan, Taiwan and Korea.

Compounding the difficulty of tracking an individual computer is the fact that several different companies—including freight consolidators at both exporting and importing ports, some located in countries distant from both buyers and sellers—are responsible for moving these goods. A recycler in Texas may well be unaware of who is unloading or receiving his goods in China or Africa. Many international freight shippers make it easy to track a whole container just punch the number into their Web site—but information about who's shipping what is not public information.

Even in Europe, where e-waste exports are regulated, illegal shipments slip through. "From our work, we have no doubt that there are improper shipments of waste," says Roy Watkinson of the U.K. Environment Agency, which in October of 2005 reported that 75 percent of the containers it had inspected that month contained some illegal waste, including e-scrap. A European group, IMPEL, a network of environmental regulators, has been monitoring this trade, and has found ships loaded with damaged computer equipment sailing out of Wales bound for Pakistan in containers marked "plastics."

According to accounts by Lai Yun of Greenpeace China and Mark Dallura of Chase Electronics in Philadelphia, and news reports from China, corruption is common among customs officials there. Dallura told the *Washington Post* in 2003 that he ships discarded computers to China via Taiwanese middlemen. "I sell it to [the Taiwanese] in Los Angeles and how they get it there is not my concern," Dallura said. "They pay the customs officials off. Everybody knows it. They show up with Mercedeses, rolls of hundred-dollar bills. This is not small-time. This is big-time stuff. There's a lot of money going on in this." Today, loads of e-scrap continue to enter the country despite the Chinese government's official crackdown on these imports. . . .

E-Waste Legislation Is Needed

The U.S. may be one of the world's biggest consumers of high-tech electronics, but unlike the European Union [EU] or Japan, the U.S. has no national system for handling e-waste. Unless a state or local government prohibits it, it's currently legal to dump up to 220 pounds a month of e-waste, including CRTs and circuit boards, into local landfills. Several dozen states have introduced e-waste bills, and a handful of U.S. states—California, Maine, Maryland, Massachusetts, Minnesota, Washington—have recently passed substantive e-waste bills, some of which bar CRTs from their landfills. E-waste bills have also been introduced in the House and Senate, but neither would create a national collection system.

The export of e-waste has been discussed in Congress but no legislation to regulate this trade has yet been introduced. Matt Gerien, press secretary to Rep. Mike Thompson, D-Calif., who has co-sponsored an e-waste bill in the House, says, "Ironically, what brought Representative Thompson to this issue are these export problems." But neither the bill that Rep. Thompson has co-sponsored with Rep. Louise Slaughter, D-N.Y., nor the one introduced by Sens. Ron Wyden, D-Ore., and Jim Talent, R-Mo., would deal with exports.

Meanwhile, says Laura Coughlan of the EPA's Office of Solid Waste, the Bush administration has drafted legislation that would allow the U.S. to ratify the Basel Convention, but is waiting for final clearance for transmittal to Congress. And the Ban amendment, which essentially prohibits sending e-waste from wealthy to poorer countries, "has created issues for U.S. ratification of the convention," says Coughlan, who explains that no "U.S. administration has supported ratification of this amendment, and the U.S. government has been unable to reach consensus with domestic stakeholders."

Legislation in Europe has made electronics recycling mandatory throughout the E.U., as it is in Japan and some other countries. Companion legislation requires the elimination of certain toxics—among them lead, cadmium and hexavalent chromium used in solder, batteries, inks and paints—from electronic products, and given the global nature of the high-tech industry, these new materials standards could effectively become world standards. Many such changes have already been made and more are in the works, but the old equipment now being discarded remains laden with toxics.

As U.S. lawmakers, manufacturers, environmental advocates, waste haulers and recyclers struggle to find a way to collect the nation's high-tech trash, Americans are left with what policymakers are fond of calling a patchwork of regulations and recycling options. This makes things as confusing for manufacturers as it does for consumers and recyclers. "At some point, the 'feds' will have to step in and harmonize things," says Ted Smith of the Silicon Valley Toxics Coalition.

In 2005, the EPA held an electronics recycling summit. Among the issues participants grappled with, and on which there is no industrywide or national policy, are that of certifying electronics recyclers and exporting electronic waste. Complaints were voiced about the difficulty of dealing with products designed with materials that make recycling complicated and expensive. But loudest of all were complaints that the U.S. had too many confusing and uncoordinated recycling efforts. A year later, a few more state laws regulating e-waste have been passed but little else has been done to stop the steady stream of used computers, cellphones and TVs that are ending up overseas, in dumps, polluting soil, water and air.

FIVE

Recyclers and Governments Are Tackling the E-Waste Problem

Andrew K. Burger

Andrew K. Burger is an Encino, California–based writer for *TechNewsWorld,* an online technology and business journal of the ECT News Network. In the following viewpoint Burger argues that manufacturers, recyclers, and governments are starting to make headway against the 87.5 percent of e-waste that currently ends up in landfills or incinerators. According to Burger, the problem calls for different solutions at different stages of the high-tech electronic product's life cycle. Manufacturers are expanding take-back programs, recycling their own electronics and printer cartridges, and finding alternatives to PVC [polyvinyl chloride] and brominated flame-retardant components. Governments are cracking down on illegal offshore scrap shipping and passing e-waste recycling laws. Individual consumers are increasingly returning their old electronics to the seller instead of throwing them in the trash. And recyclers are developing new, safer ways to recover rare earth and base metals and reprocess transformers, circuit boards, and monitors that contain PCBs [polychlorinated biphenyl] and hazardous heavy metals.

Part 1: Exporting Toxic Waste

(January 3, 2008) While they are instrumental in disseminating information and raising environmental consciousness, our dependence on digital electronics is also putting ever greater strains on us and our environment.

"Manufacturing a desktop computer and 17-inch CRT monitor uses at least 240 kg (530 lbs) of fossil fuels, 22 kg (50 lbs) of chemicals and 1,500 kg (3,330 lbs) of water—a total of 1.8 tons (1.9 English tons) of materials—roughly the weight of a sports utility vehicle or a rhinoceros," according to *Computers and the Environment*, a 2004 book released by United Nations University (UNU).

While mountains of e-waste continue to accumulate in dump sites and landfills around the world, establishing viable electronics recycling programs worldwide is slow going. It's a colossal task that requires long-term commitments from all parties that make up the life cycle of any laptop, PC or electronic product, not the least of which is the consumer. . . .

A Vexing Problem

Almost all laptops and PCs in the U.S. are simply thrown in the trash, leaving governments, aid agencies and taxpaying consumers to pick up the costs—monetary, environmental and ultimately those related to health care. The Environmental Protection Agency (EPA) estimates that in 2005 only 330,000 pounds, or 12.5 percent, of the 2.63 million tons of electronic waste that was disposed was recovered for recycling. The other 87.5 percent ended up in landfills or incinerators. Exactly how they are being recycled is a large, thorny and troubling problem in and of itself.

More fundamentally, making a truly eco-friendly notebook, laptop or PC just isn't possible, certainly not at the present time. "My usual answer is rather simple: We will never have a green PC or laptop. It's a high tech product—just keeping in mind how much energy and resources are needed to produce, use and then dispose of and recycle them—but we must ensure that they are designed, built and disposed of in ways that are environmentally sound. We need to establish a type of competition to develop ecologically sound products and processes. . . . Thermodynamically and technically it's possible, but it's not economically feasible," maintained Ruediger Kuehr at the United Nations University in Bonn, Germany, and a coauthor of *Computers and the Environment*. . . .

Creative, Coordinated Problem Solving

Changing "business as usual" and consumer mindsets that include every person in the world who purchases a laptop or piece of electronic equipment isn't simple, or cheap. It's a product life cycle loop that encompasses manufacturers, extends across transnational supply chains through retailers to every consumer in every nation and then on to those involved in collecting, recycling, reusing and disposing of e-waste and e-scrap.

Progress is being made, however. HP [Hewlett-Packard] has been running its own recycling program for 20 years. It has take-back programs in more than 40 countries. Going forward, it aims to double its annual recovery rate and reach the 2 billion pound electronics and printer cartridge recycling mark by year-end 2010. The company [in 2007] met an initial goal set in 2004 of recycling 1 billion pounds of electronics.

HP in 2006 recovered 187 million pounds of electronics globally, 73 percent more than IBM, its closest competitor. "Environmental responsibility is good business," said Mark Hurd, HP chairman and chief executive officer. "We've reached the tipping point where the price and performance of IT [information technology] are no longer compromised by being green, but are now enhanced by it."

Operationally, HP's extensive list of environmental goals for [2007] included continuing to divert 87 percent of solid, nonhazardous waste from landfills globally and finding alternatives to the use of brominated flame retardants and PVC (polyvinyl chloride) in external case plastic parts of all new HP brand product models introduced after Dec. 31, 2006.

HP's recycling initiatives extend throughout the organization and beyond. Gathering accurate and timely data on product life cycles and materials and energy usage is the first and most critical step. It's in the process of assessing them for 95 percent of product materials, components, manufacturing and transportation suppliers by number and by spend.

Initial phases of employee training programs in China and Central Europe were completed [in 2008]. Auditors are being trained and supplier educational programs have been conducted in Brazil, Central Europe, China, India, Southeast Asia and Vietnam. In China, HP is coleading a program to create a "capability building strategy for the electronic sector" in cooperation with the World Bank, the Chinese government and the Shenzhen Electronics Association.

Governments Taking Action

Among world governments, the EU [European Union] has been the most aggressive when it comes to taking on responsibility for tackling the e-waste and e-scrap issues. Its Waste Electrical and Electronic Equipment (WEEE) regulations went into effect on Jan. 2, 2007, but changing deeply ingrained practices at all points of the product life cycle is a very difficult nut to crack. "By law, all EU members are condemning illegal exports, but there is still quite a lot still leaving Europe as products categorized for reuse and refurbishment. . . . Shipments are difficult to distinguish for customs officers and others," explained Kuehr.

Legislative impetus is now coming to a head in the U.S. Twenty-three states introduced electronics recycling bills in 2007. "It's actually being adopted faster than I thought it would—three states over three years (2004–2006); (in 2007) five states adopted producer take-back laws for e-waste," Schneider noted.

"Electronics is really the cutting edge of producer take-back programs in the U.S. Because five bills passed, and in such diverse places—California, Texas, Connecticut, Minnesota and North Carolina—this year it became clear that's the way we're going," she continued. "State and local governments made a big difference; they realize they cannot afford all the costs and problems associated with e-waste and we've convinced the major electronics companies to support that. . . . The bill here in Texas was drafted by Dell and supported by HP after we did corporate campaigning and pressured them since 2002."

State E-Waste Laws and Bills Under Consideration for 2008

States enacting recycling laws use two basic models: (1) The producer responsibility model, requiring manufacturers to pay for collection and recycling of their products, and (2) the Advanced Recycling Fee (ARF) model, in which consumers are charged a recycling fee when buying a product. The ARF fees go into a statewide recycling fund, which is used to reimburse recycling costs.

States that have passed e-waste laws		States with bills under consideration in 2008		
Producer responsibility	ARF consumer fees laws	Producer responsibility	ARF bills	Both

Taken from: Electronics Take-Back Coalition, "State E-Waste Laws and Bills Under Consideration for 2008," 2008. www.w-takeback.org.

Closing the Loop

Adding to the momentum, the concepts of expanded, or individual, producer responsibility and "Cradle to Cradle" product and process design are gaining traction. Industry participants are devoting more resources and finding ways to recycle and reuse materials.

Developing the concepts entails establishing the market structure and incentives that result in "producers competing not only on the basis of how fast and how well they can manufacture their products, but how fast and how well they can recycle them," Schneider maintained.

Such creative environmental problem solving is also leading researchers and policy advisors to evaluate the idea of "product dematerialization."

"The ideal case from my point of view would be that the customer would not purchase the product but purchase the service for, say, a one-, two- or three-year period. . . . It is then returned to the manufacturer and the consumer is issued a new one, thereby closing the loop," Kuehr explained.

"In this way, it's in the interest of the assembler to make the most of the product's return. . . . I can see various positive effects from the dematerialization of electronic equipment—it would ensure the sharp progress of technologies, even shortening new product introduction periods. . . . There's been some testing of new products by large OEMs (original equipment manufacturers) on these issues, but there's no information as to how in-depth they were. There does not seem to be any attractive way of dealing with these problems, which makes it easier to continue business as usual. . . . This is visionary, not a one- or two-year effort, but mid- to long-term planning," he said. . . .

Part 2: Doing the Job Right

(*January 10, 2008*) Consider another situation: [Hypothetical] laptop owner Joe Verdi doesn't own a laptop from a brand name OEM with a take-back program. He wants to recycle it and he gets lucky, or is clued-in about the shady global trade in e-waste, and he finds an honest, ethical PC recycler in his area that's going to do the job right. The laptop will likely follow a similar path if it's turned into any of the take-back, recycling programs run by major laptop manufacturers.

The laptop will likely be reconditioned and sold second-hand or broken down for parts rather than recycled. That's the main reason costs to recyclers and prices to laptop owners turning their machines in at recycling centers are lower than they otherwise would be.

"There still is a fair amount of residual value in laptops—they are in higher demand. We charge about US$2.50 to process a laptop—a little below the market average, but we get so many," explained Jeremy Farber, president of PC Recycler.

"Only 20 percent are actually recycled; the rest get reconditioned and reused," he added. "We work with a couple of companies that reuse the parts, even plastic casing," he added.

Down the Recycling Stream

If it's recycled in the U.S. rather than reused or exported overseas for dismantling and dumping, Joe's laptop will wind up at an independent recycling shop or in an OEM's (original equipment manufacturer) in-house recycling program.

With centers in Virginia and New York, PC Recycler is one of many recyclers whose business is increasing as consumers become more environmentally conscious and investments in new businesses and recycling value chains gain market traction. Though the company, which is privately held, doesn't disclose revenues, Farber said PC Recycler's business grew 160 percent by weight of PCs processed year over year.

The OEMs exert a big influence on the profitability of independent recyclers, according to Farber. For one thing, large OEMs' in-house recycling programs compete with independent recyclers. In addition, each manufacturer has its own particular design, parts and assembly specifications, which add to the difficulty and cost of recycling laptops to independent recyclers. "You can't process a laptop mechanically; you have to manually remove a few components," Farber elaborated.

For instance, laptops' circuit boards and plastic casings are treated with potentially toxic brominated flame retardants. Transformers and capacitors contain PCBs (polychlorinated biphenyls), and monitors and other devices are chock full of a host of heavy metals, including lead, zinc, cadmium and chromium. Their lighting contains mercury, which qualifies as a hazardous material. Similarly, batteries have to be treated as hazardous waste. "These have to be removed and shredded, and that's complicated," Farber said. "You can't just start shredding laptops; those mercury lights have to come out."

"The manufacturers don't make it easy—they use nonstandard configurations. They're manufactured different ways by different

A Hewlett-Packard worker at the company's recycling center in Roseville, California, removes hazardous materials from a computer before separating and shredding the different materials.

manufacturers; the assembly is completely different, so that forces us to have a higher standard worker and process to recycle them," Farber continued.

Recovering Rare and Precious Metals

Precious, rare earth and base metals—such as indium, lithium, bismuth, ruthenium, platinum, nickel and gold—are essential to producing PCs, and prices for them have been rising dramatically in recent years. Their higher prices, along with advances in recapturing them from e-waste and the development of a supporting recycling industry value chain, is making recycling more economically feasible. Attracting sufficiently high volumes is the key to market success, however.

The price of indium—a compound that is used in making flat screens and more than a billion products per year—has increased six-fold in the last five years, making it more expensive than silver. While known mine reserves are limited, indium recycling has been taking place in a few plants in Belgium, Japan and the U.S. Japan recovers roughly half its indium needs through recycling, according to the United Nations University (UNU), home of the UN Solving the E-Waste Problem (StEP) initiative's secretariat.

"The large price spikes for all these special elements that rely on production of metals like zinc, copper, lead or platinum underline that supply security at affordable prices cannot be guaranteed indefinitely unless efficient recycling loops are established to recover them from old products," UNU professor Ruediger Kuehr stated.

SIX

Curbside Recycling Increases When People Do Not Have to Sort Their Trash

Susan Kinsella

In the following viewpoint, recycled-paper expert Susan Kinsella, the author of *The Single-Stream Best Practices Manual*, assesses the impact of single-stream curbside recycling programs, the hottest trend in U.S. municipal solid waste management. According to Kinsella, consumers are more likely to recycle when they can put all their paper, bottles, cans, and plastic in one curbside bin, and collectors can put fewer trucks on the road since all-in-one pickup is more efficient. Sorting technology at material recovery facilities (MRFs) does need improvement so recycled content is purer (paper, glass, and plastic do not contaminate each other), but the good news is that single-stream communities are reporting that as much as 49.5 percent of their trash is now kept out of landfills. Susan Kinsella is executive director of Conservatree, a San Francisco nonprofit that provides technical assistance and information on environmentally sound papers for individual, small-scale, and professional paper buyers.

Susan Kinsella, "Single-Stream: Closing the Loop," *Resource Recycling*, vol. 25, January 2006, pp. 12–18. Reproduced by permission.

Why are single-stream collection and processing recycling programs so attractive to some and so problematic to others? Clearly the popularity of single-stream programs is rapidly changing the nature of recycling in North America but, at the same time, single-stream might be more accurately perceived as but one response to a series of challenges and opportunities.

The public is not aware of the sea changes happening in their community recycling programs, including single-stream collection and processing, landfill diversion to the exclusion of other recycling goals, and reliance on exports, but even many within the industry are unaware of the details. Surprisingly, little long-term thinking has accompanied these changes, in part perhaps because recycling is a very present-oriented activity:

- Materials are discarded every day and collected within very short timeframes.
- Processors generally need to clear out their facilities every day to be ready for the next day's materials.
- Manufacturers need recovered material on hand to continually feed their equipment.

Beyond these daily activities, recycling is also a system that needs long-term planning and consideration in order to keep its immediate functions effectively operating. Recycling is a collaborative system: manufacturers need the material that collectors collect and processors process, and collectors and processors need manufacturers who buy their materials. As such, recycling needs to be reviewed as an interdependent system to determine whether the changes occurring in North America will result in a healthy, long-term recycling system.

Recognizing the need to raise awareness about these issues, Conservatree initiated the Single-Stream Roundtable in Sacramento, in May 2005, to bring together governments, collectors, processors and manufacturers from across California to discuss the impact of single-stream recycling. Since single-stream service has become the recycling program of choice for the majority of California communities, the Golden State is a good microcosm for observation and discussions about application, implementation, implications and the potential for improvements.

Early Numbers Show Positive Results

For the most part, collectors and local governments operating single-stream programs are pleased with the results. They appreciate that it:

- Brings in more recyclables
- Increases diversion rates
- Reduces worker compensation costs
- Reduces the number of trucks on the road
- Often allows additional materials to be added to the collection system.

According to Lynn France, conservation coordinator for the City of Chula Vista, California, a state mandate for 50-percent diversion [any combination of waste reduction, recycling, composting, etc., that keeps waste out of landfills] changed the recycling landscape from a demand-side market (where shortages raise prices to increase collection) to a supply-side market (where materials are collected to keep them out of landfills, not in response to a market demand). The continuous volume and lack of reference to price signals lowered prices, undermined processors' concern for quality end-products and facilitated many communities' move to single-stream.

Chula Vista converted as source-separation curbside recycling collection program to single-stream with automated collection in 2002. The new single-stream program continued collecting the same commodities—paper, bottles, cans and plastics, with yard waste collected separately—but now required participants to load all their recyclables into one 32-, 64- or 96-gallon cart rather than an 18-gallon bin, paper bags and a trash container. The city also implemented a variable-rate structure that provided an incentive for participants to divert more materials that had previously been going into the trash.

France says recycling volumes have increased by 100 percent. Interestingly, the increase occurred during an improving economy and did not reduce trash volumes. The program now has an average seven-percent residue rate compared to its previous two-percent rate.

Advanced Technology Makes Single-Stream Recycling More Efficient

Eddy-current separator

1. A stream of waste material travels along a conveyor belt.

3. A secondary magnetic field is induced in metallic items, and magnetic repulsion pushes them clear of the waste stream.

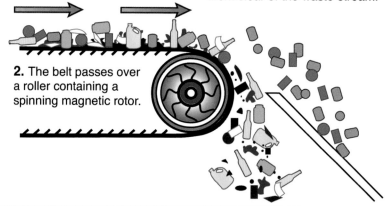

2. The belt passes over a roller containing a spinning magnetic rotor.

Spectroscopic sorter

1. A stream of waste material travels along a conveyor belt and passes under a camera.

2. Each type of material reflects a unique combination of wavelengths in the infrared spectrum and can thus be identified.

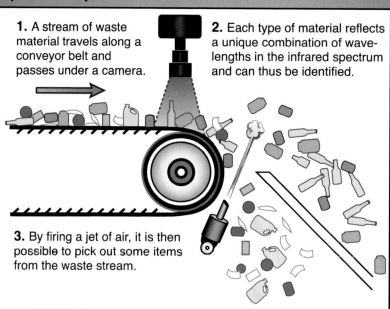

3. By firing a jet of air, it is then possible to pick out some items from the waste stream.

Taken from: TiTech and the *Economist*, "The Truth About Recycling," June 7, 2007.

San Jose—long recognized for its high-quality, multi-sort recycling program—also produced positive results following a challenging start-up. After a difficult first year, including a nearly five-fold increase in its residue rate, averaging 30 percent, and a decrease in diversion, the city has seen single-family recycling tonnages increase by 25 percent and diversion by 11.5 percent over the prior source-separated system. San Jose's residential diversion rate is now at an all-time high of 49.5 percent.

As previously mentioned, San Jose encountered significant challenges en route to its high diversion rate and learned some valuable lessons. It learned, for example, that pay-as-you-throw systems can encourage residents to put extra garbage in recycling carts to avoid higher garbage fees. Additionally, large, 96-gallon recycling carts provide contamination opportunities as drivers cannot see the materials as they are picked-up.

Most critically, San Jose learned that contract incentives can make single-stream programs more effective, but only when subcontractors' terms also reflect those incentives and the city maintains control of the materials stream. Because collection efficiencies and higher diversion rates trade off for higher contamination, single-stream programs also require a greater focus on outreach programs and more work at the material recovery facility (MRF) to effectively sort materials.

Identifying Problems

For others, especially many recycled-product manufacturers, single-stream programs are more problematic. The most commonly cited troubles are:

- Poor quality feedstocks
- Reduced energy efficiencies
- Increased internal costs
- Lost access to recyclables
- Landfilling of significant percentages of feedstock materials.

California and West Coast recycled-product manufacturers value the volume promised by single-stream collection and processing programs, but they say the quality issues they are experiencing may limit their ability to maintain and expand markets for recycled-content products.

Many from local community recycling programs attending the Roundtable were astonished to learn that significant percentages of the recyclables they counted as diverted end up landfilled— not recycled—at manufacturing plants because they are so poorly sorted. Since more than 75 percent of curbside collection is paper fiber, paper mills are hardest-hit, with plastics, glass and metals all ending up in their recovered fiber bales.

Les Joel, deink plant superintendent for Blue Heron Paper Co. (Oregon City, Oregon), has seen the mill make a number of equipment and process improvements to account for the trend towards single-stream recycling, but the impact is still daunting. . . .

Contaminants such as glass, for example, require expensive screen baskets to be replaced twice as often, nearly doubling annual replacement costs. Meanwhile, the glass, metals and plastics introduced into the papermaking system by poor MRF sorting wear out pipes and pumps more quickly. . . .

Improving Sorting Quality

Not only are plastics, glass and metal cans serious problems at paper mills, they also are contaminants at other types of manufacturing facilities. Plastics manufacturers are receiving glass while glass manufacturers are receiving unsorted glass mixed with paper fibers and non-cullet contaminants. But the biggest concern for plastics and glass manufacturers is all the recyclables lost to their own recycled-product manufacturing because they were delivered instead to paper mills.

"If you're not using the material diverted, you didn't divert," said Dennis Sabourin, executive director of NAPCOR (Sonoma, California). Paper mills say that 39 million pounds of plastics were sent to their mills in one year because of poor sorting. Though the generating communities counted that tonnage in their diversion rate, it actually just took a longer route to the landfill.

Sabourin agreed that single-stream recycling, if done properly, will work, but it requires proper techniques and capital expendi-

PET bottles get recycled at a German plant. The value of recycled PET plastics is four to five times greater than that of recycled newspapers.

tures. MRF equipment is expensive, ranging from $1 to $6 million per plant, but can increase processing production to up to 40 tons per hour. Screening and optical equipment have been improving auto-separation of materials and making sorting easier for line workers.

With PET plastics, solving single-stream's problems is economically compelling. While the value of one metric ton of newsprint is between $100 and $125, the value of the same weight of PET is $530 to $570. And in California, where containers earn a container redemption value plus processing payments, one metric ton of PET is worth $2,066.

Tom Mabie, West Coast counsel for the Glass Packaging Institute (Alexandria, Virginia), also insisted, "Diversion is not the same as recycling." Over-emphasis on diversion has resulted in some local communities not paying attention to the implications of choosing low cost programs. . . .

Taking a Systemic Approach

The challenges single-stream recycling presents are not isolated to individual sectors. From collection to processing to manufacturing, each sector faces issues that must be overcome for the system to work as a whole.

At the community level, increased public education is a critical factor for a program's success. When transitioning to single-stream collection, San Jose committed over $2 million to outreach efforts and continues spending over $350,000 per year in on-going education. A city also can improve material quality through contract management.

Peter Slote, recycling specialist with the City of Oakland, believes that single-stream's impact on product quality is less affected by contamination from non-program materials by residents than by cross-contamination of acceptable materials during processing, especially when materials flow into large, regional single-stream facilities handling materials from multiple jurisdictions.

Tom Mabie suggests dealing with contamination at the collection and processing stage by ending compaction in collection vehicles and initiating a first, positive sort for glass at the MRF. Blue Heron has taken steps at the mill to deal with contamination by modernizing equipment, adding a drum pulper as well as more cleaners and screens. The mill also plans another $3 million in upgrades to its contaminant removal process and is looking at ways of decreasing landfilling costs by using plastics and inappropriate fibers as a fuel source.

Government participants at all levels suggested getting millage loss reports from the manufacturers who receive their recovered materials, in order to evaluate their processors' effectiveness and calculate true diversion rates that take into account whether their materials were actually recycled. They also recognized the importance of including recycled-product manufacturers in feedback loops for designing and evaluating their programs.

Increased volumes are good, increased participation is good and material quality is a problem. With budgets getting tighter and waste streams growing, it seems clear that more communities see single-stream as worth the trade-offs, but how long will those trade-offs work if recycling is not addressed as a whole system? Recycling's inherent interdependency means that problems in one sector will eventually undermine gains in other sectors.

Most Roundtable participants agreed, though, that single-stream recycling can fulfill its promise if local communities' recycling programs require quality as well as quantity. As Pat DeRueda, president of Waste Management/Recycle America Alliance (Houston), the nation's largest collector and processor of municipal recyclables, put it, "We've just got to make sure that what's going into the bales is meeting the specs of the mills." Simple, right?

SEVEN

Curbside Recycling Works Better When People Presort Their Trash

Brian Taylor

Brian Taylor is editor in chief of *Recycling Today*, a monthly business magazine that covers the commodity processing and recycling industry. In the following viewpoint, Taylor argues that single-stream recycling programs are far less efficient than material recovery facilities (MRFs) would like consumers to believe. Even when processing plants are retooled to accept unsorted trash streams of mixed paper, plastic, and glass, Taylor says, the end product after on-site sorting is low-quality material that buyers such as paperboard mills do not want. Too much recycled fiber is contaminated with glass powder that wrecks recycled-paper mills' equipment. Even worse, he warns, consumers get lazy when they think all they have to do is toss their trash into a single container: People put unrecyclable garbage in the mix, too, and neglect to clean even recyclable material first. Presorting at the curb makes the recycling process much more efficient.

Brian Taylor, "Dual Purposes," *Recycling Today*, vol. 41, June 1, 2003, pp. 48, 50, 52–53. www.Recycling Today.com.

Single-stream recycling collection and processing has marched steadily forward, and no one is more aware than Mark Naef of Naef Recycling, East Syracuse, N.Y.

Naef started his company [in 2002] to handle commercial and residential recyclables collected in and around Syracuse. Residential collection and processing in that area has traditionally been done in the dual-stream manner, with fibers segregated from the container stream. The Naef Recycling plant was set up to process materials collected that way.

But no sooner had Naef Recycling opened its doors than Waste Management Inc., Houston, set up some of its first single-stream programs in the eastern U.S. at new material recovery facilities (MRFs) in Syracuse and Binghamton, N.Y. Naef says the introduction of single-stream techniques has sent mixed signals to haulers and municipalities in the region, and if it is ultimately a stronger signal that mixing materials is fine, then he may have to change the way he does business.

Single-Stream Produces Poor-Quality Raw Material

Single-stream equipment makers and MRF operators are confident that plants can be set up to produce quality fiber streams from material collected through the single-stream method.

But Naef contends that mills he sells to, such as the Abitibi-Consolidated mill in Thorold, Ontario, Canada, or the Solvay Paperboard mills in New York, can tell when they are seeing single-stream material because of the increased presence of glass pieces and glass powder.

The glass powder is difficult to spot on visual inspections, but Naef says the effect of the contaminant becomes clear over time. "The powder is practically sand-blasting the equipment it comes in contact with at mills," he remarks.

Additional contaminants such as lids from steel cans and plastic bags, caps and rings are also common in many single-stream shipments, Naef contends.

While he understands the desire for municipalities and haulers to reduce their collection costs, he wonders whether they realize that they are losing money on the selling end of the transaction. He says the nearby single-stream MRF operated by Waste Management is shipping out numerous loads of the "hard-pack" mixed low-grade of paper, while his MRF produces only one or two bales per month of this commodity.

While plant operators and equipment makers devise methods to improve sorting, Naef notes that true single-stream collection is not in place until compactor trucks are doing the collecting. That's when recyclers are really put to the test to make clean, high-quality shipments. "It's a whole new dynamic," he remarks. "When they first try single stream, it's with older collection methods."

Dual-Stream Reminds People They Cannot Treat Recyclables Like Garbage

Naef acknowledges that he has several biases when looking at the dual-stream versus single-stream issue, not the least of which is that he has just opened a plant designed to handle materials collected with the dual-stream method.

He also believes that the move toward single stream is blurring the line between recyclables and garbage and undoing several years of recycling education about keeping recyclable commodities clean out of consideration for consuming mills. "My background is in the environmental movement," says Naef, "and I'm concerned we're losing the conservation component of recycling when the individual no longer has to take care of what is being recycled."

Naef says programs should continue collecting "the way it's been done for years" in Syracuse and other parts of Onondaga County, N.Y.: "Either two bins, one for bottles and one for paper, or paper in the same bin but within a bag."

He and other dual-stream advocates have publicized the advantages of dual-stream collection. This effort may eventually involve a legal challenge calling upon jurisdictions to enforce a source

Proponents say separate container recycling can increase a municipality's recycling revenues.

separation law in New York state that Naef says requires those collecting recyclables to keep materials segregated in the same method they are brought to the curb. Naef says the law's origin lies in preventing haulers from dumping recyclables into garbage trucks to take materials directly to the landfill.

"Preserving the integrity of the education message and of recycling as a separate collection process is critical," says Naef. He says there has been little opposition from residents to performing their own sorting tasks, as Onondaga County has a 95 percent recycling participation rate and a diversion rate that has been calculated in the 40 percent to 60 percent range.

Processors Scramble to Take Single-Stream Waste Without Know-How and Equipment

The single-stream collection message seems to have spread rapidly, however. Naef notes that shortly after the publicity by Waste Management that they would accept single-stream materials, he began to see more commingled materials coming his way. "They've changed the way people collect in an award-winning recycling program," he remarks.

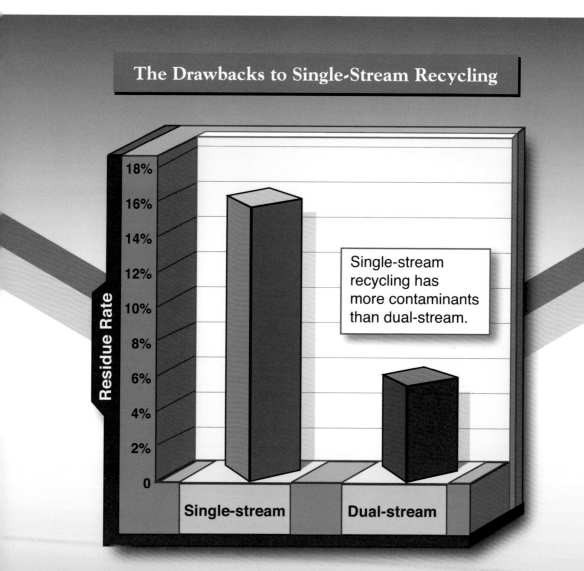

Taken from: Gershman, Brickner & Bratton, "Making Dual-Stream Recycling Better than Single-Stream," SWANA WasteCon presentation, 2005.

Currently, enough dual-stream material is coming in that Naef Recycling is still able to produce the ONP (old newspaper) grades it strives for, but since 2003, he has noticed a greater influx of single-stream material being tipped at his MRF.

"Eventually, I may try an incentive system, such as not charging haulers who bring in dual-stream materials, but charging a tip fee for single-stream materials," says Naef.

There are several signs that despite Naef's best efforts, the single-stream tide is not ebbing. In a session on the topic at the Federation of New York Solid Waste Associations conference in Bolton's Landing, N.Y., in early May [2003], several speakers commented on the status of single-stream recycling.

Eileen Berenyi of Governmental Advisory Associates, Westport, Conn., publishers of the Materials Recycling and Processing in the United States directory, noted that the number of MRFs claiming to process single-stream materials jumped from a dozen or less in 1995 to 78 by 2001, with that number having grown to as much as 90 currently.

At the time she conducted her survey, Berenyi found that 57 percent of the single-stream plants were in the western U.S., 30 percent in the South, 13 percent in the Midwest and none in the Northeast. But subsequently, Waste Management has opened its two single-stream plants in New York, with other installations and conversions also taking place in the northeastern U.S. and just across the border in Canada, where Haycore Canada Inc. operates two single-stream plants. . . .

Theodore Pytlar of Dvirka & Bartilucci Engineers, S. Plainfield, N.J., and Nat Egosi of RRT Design & Construction, Melville, N.Y., each noted that operators were finding different reasons to gravitate toward single-stream set-ups.

Pytlar noted that MRFs want to lower labor costs by using automated equipment, with screens such as the Lubo StarScreen gaining popularity because of their ability to let glass fall through early in the process, thus protecting conveyors and balers from handling glass (and keeping paper grades cleaner).

According to Egosi, single-stream automated MRFs are also allowing facilities to handle more material, with operators in the western U.S. having grown accustomed to the process and having learned how to lower residue rates. He noted additionally, though, that the slower economy with its tight municipal and state budgets may slow down the trend from growing in the eastern U.S. for awhile. . . .

Kevin Roche of the Broome County Department of Solid Waste, Binghamton, N.Y., which has worked with Waste Management Inc. to open the single-stream MRF in that city, . . . said that the MRF has exceeded the county's performance expectations in terms of keeping residue rates low and for increasing material collected. "Single-stream recycling can work; it's a matter of whether you're ready for it," he stated.

Converting to Single-Stream Probably Means No More Glass Recycling

Steven N. Stein of GBB Inc., Fairfax, Va., outlined a connection between residue rates and handling glass in several cases studied by the consulting firm. When tailoring recycling programs for cities and solid waste authorities, his firm has increasingly advocated dropping glass from programs. The material now accounts for only 3 percent of the municipal solid waste (MSW) stream, versus 10 percent in 1970, so its diversion value has decreased greatly. When it does show up at MRFs, its harmful qualities (contaminating loads of other commodities and its abrasiveness against equipment) greatly outweigh any diversion rate boosts or market value, said Stein.

Stein said messages from recycled paper consumers such as SP Newsprint, Dublin, Ga. (a sizable consumer of ONP), that it would consider switching a secondary fiber-consuming mill to wood chips if recyclers can't control contamination problems should be a clear signal to MRF operators to keep plastic, metals and glass out of fiber loads.

Naef believes he is on the same side as the mills, but he is not certain that the trend toward single-stream collecting and processing can be reversed. Currently, Naef says there is still enough dual-stream material coming in to keep his plant viable. But if the single-stream collection method ultimately prevails, he may find himself facing sorting and separating challenges he never intended to tackle.

EIGHT

Curbside Recycling Increases in Pay-as-You-Throw Communities

Janice Canterbury and Sue Eisenfeld

Even people who have never heard the phrase "pay as you throw" (PAYT) still recognize a growing trend in waste collection across America: Instead of paying a flat fee for weekly trash removal, no matter how much or how little trash there is to pick up, residents now pay by the size of the trash can or the number of bags of trash they generate. In the following viewpoint Janice Canterbury and Sue Eisenfeld argue that PAYT is a proven incentive to divert waste from the garbage can to the recycle bin. According to the authors, PAYT communities are reducing waste collection by up to 35 percent and increasing recycling rates to more than 55 percent. Canterbury is the PAYT program manager at the Environmental Protection Agency in Washington, D.C. Eisenfeld is a senior environmental communications manager with Eastern Research Group, an environmental consulting firm in Arlington, Virginia.

Communities with pay-as-you-throw (PAYT) programs charge residents for the collection of MSW [municipal solid waste] based on the amount they throw away. [According to the EPA (Environmental Protection Agency), MSW includes "packaging, grass clipping, furniture, clothing, bottles, food scraps, newspapers,

Janice Canterbury, Sue Eisenfeld, "The Rise and . . . Rise of Pay-As-You-Throw," *MSW Management Elements*, vol. 15, 2006. Reproduced by permission.

appliances, paint, and batteries."] This creates a direct economic incentive to generate less waste and compost and recycle more.

Traditionally, residents pay for waste collection through property taxes or a fixed fee, regardless of how much—or how little—trash they generate. PAYT breaks with tradition by treating trash services just like electricity, gas, and other utilities. Households pay a variable rate depending on the amount of service they use.

Communities usually offer bags, tags, or cans as part of a PAYT program, and they charge residents for trash in a number of different ways:

- *Proportional:* Residents are charged the same amount of money for each unit they set out for collection (e.g., $1.50 for each 30-gallon bag).
- *Variable:* Residents are charged a different amount per different-size units of garbage to which they subscribe (e.g., 32- to 64-gallon containers). Subsequent containers cost extra.
- *Two-Tiered or Multitiered:* Residents subscribe to a base level of service, for which they pay a flat fee. They then pay a second-tier fee based on the amount of waste they set out, either variable or proportional.

From 1916 to 2004, the number of communities implementing pay-as-you-throw (PAYT) programs has grown exponentially, from just one (Richmond, CA) to more than 6,000.

You know it's not a passing trend when it's been written about in major industry and economic journals since the 1970s. Another clue that it has legitimacy is that more and more communities are adopting it each year, in the United States and internationally. You get a pretty good sense of the depth and breadth of its effectiveness when you realize that towns and cities of all sizes in every region of the country have adopted it, tailoring it to their own unique circumstances and needs. And you know it's not just being embraced for its feel-good, tree-hugging qualities when you see the millions of dollars communities are saving because of it. There's no doubt about it: PAYT, also known as unit-based or variable pricing, is a tried and true approach for meeting a variety of MSW management goals.

How Common Is Pay-as-You-Throw in Your State?

Number of Communities with Pay-as-You-Throw

| 0 | 1–25 | 26–100 | 101–200 | 200+ |

Taken from: Skumatz Economic Research Associates, PAYT surveys, 2005–2006.

PAYT Success Stories

Trade journal articles and reports from the last decade document the phenomenal success PAYT has had in saving money, reducing waste, and increasing recyclables. For example:

- Gainesville, FL (pop. 95,500), saved $200,000 in landfill tipping fees after implementing PAYT in 1994, reduced solid waste collection by 18%, and increased its recycling rate by about 25%.

- Wilmington, NC (pop. 75,800), saved $400,000 in the first year of PAYT (1992).
- Worcester, MA (pop. 172,600), decreased its waste management costs by $1.2 million and increased its recycling rate from 3% to 36% immediately following the introduction of PAYT in 1993.

Communities with pay-as-you-throw garbage collection have realized savings in money, reduced waste, increased recyclables, and landfill space.

- The recycling rate in San Jose, CA (pop. 895,000), rose from 28% to 43% in the first year of its program (1993), and rose again to 55% by 1998.
- In Tacoma, WA (pop. 194,000), solid waste management costs fell by more than 50% in the PAYT program's first year, and the recycling rate tripled.
- Falmouth, ME (pop. 4,100), decreased its trash disposal volume by 35% and increased recycling by more than 50% after establishing PAYT in 1992.
- In Mount Vernon, IA (pop. 3,400), PAYT helped the community reach a 50% recycling rate.

Whether due to a landfill closing or to the need to meet state or local recycling goals or mandates, or because it's simply the right thing to do, communities nationwide have found that PAYT leads them toward solutions. . . .

Massachusetts Takes a Voluntary Approach

Some states, like Iowa, Minnesota, Washington, and Wisconsin, require PAYT through mandates to ensure that financial incentives for waste reduction are implemented, but other states, like Massachusetts, encourage PAYT as a voluntary measure. This latter approach seems to be working: 110 out of 351 cities and towns in Massachusetts have implemented PAYT as of October 2004.

In Massachusetts, PAYT has been implemented in communities with fewer than 300 residents and in large urban areas of close to 200,000. Each community has tailored its PAYT program to its circumstances: 57 communities use a bag system, 36 communities use stickers, 7 communities allow residents to use their own receptacle and pay by container, 5 communities use punch cards, 2 municipalities have a franchise system, and 2 communities use more than one system. In terms of rate systems, communities also range widely in how they decided to bill residents: 8 communities use proportional rates, 9 communities use variable rates, 58 communities use two-tiered rates, and 34 use multitiered rates. More than half of these communities show a recycling rate of 40% or greater (compared to 31% in non-PAYT communities). And residents in PAYT communities dispose of 8.8% less garbage than those in non-PAYT communities. . . .

Massachusetts began offering grants to municipalities for new PAYT programs in 1996, and three municipalities qualified for the grant in the first year. In 1997, Massachusetts instituted a challenge grant program, which provided incentive payments to qualifying municipalities for each ton of recyclables collected. Eligibility for payments was based on a menu of criteria, one of which was implementing a PAYT program. During the heyday of this grant program, 29 communities adopted PAYT.

What's the key to the state's success? Education. Lambert has held more than 50 municipal trainings, workshops, and videoconferences over the past 10 years, which have reached an estimated 1,000 solid waste managers, elected officials, and community volunteers, who then better understand the value of PAYT and how it works. . . .

To Each His Own in Maine

Like Massachusetts, more than 100 communities throughout the state of Maine have adopted PAYT. But unlike its Northeast neighbor, Maine does not provide any incentives to do so and does not provide a comprehensive "how to" educational program. While the state does provide some PAYT tools and information on its Web site, these communities have turned to PAYT on their own as a solution to financial problems. "PAYT is not a feel-green kind of thing here; it's a financial thing," explains Tom Miragliuolo, a planner with the Maine State Planning Office.

The first PAYT community started in the late 1980s; through 2002, nine new communities per year, amounting to 137 communities representing 296,000 Mainers, or 23% of the state's population, have started using PAYT. The average size of a PAYT town is 2,162 people, with Portland as the largest community with 65,000 people. Most started using PAYT as a solution to high tipping fees and see PAYT as a method to reduce trash generation and associated disposal fees, while also increasing recycling.

With a few exceptions, all of the programs use some form of bag or tag system, charging between $0.30 and $2 per bag of trash. Thirty towns offer different-size bags; Falmouth, for example, offers a 15-gallon bag for $0.64 and a 33-gallon bag for $0.91. Twenty-seven communities use a weight-based system. Maine also has four privately run PAYT programs, where it is up to the residents to contact a private hauler and arrange for trash removal. One program, in Durham, provides residents with 26 free bags per year; additional bags cost $3 each. . . .

A College Town Learning Curve in Athens, OH

With high populations of young and seemingly motivated and environmentally conscious individuals, college towns are, in some ways, the perfect place for PAYT. In Austin, TX (University of Texas), Tompkins County, NY (Cornell University and Ithaca College), Boulder and Fort Collins, CO (University of Colorado and Colorado State University), Athens-Clarke County, GA (University of Georgia), and other college towns across the nation, PAYT programs thrive. But behind the scenes, these communities face many unique challenges, such as varied living arrangements and an extremely transient population.

In Athens, OH, 20,000 of the 25,000 residents are Ohio University students, many of whom live off-campus in the community. Seventy percent of Athens's households are rental units—the vast majority of which are seasonal or temporary, based on the university calendar. Also, because most occupants are not homeowners, they are not necessarily invested in maintaining their neighborhoods. Constant household changes create significant communication problems, as residents aren't aware of community policies regarding recycling and solid waste reduction measures. . . .

To overcome these hurdles, officials in Athens have worked overtime to inform and educate the students and other residents. By creating and distributing information packets, developing a sample lease agreement for landlords to assist in laying out the laws and regulations, and increasing enforcement of solid waste regulations, the community has been able to make PAYT work.

The seeds to Athens's success were planted early by developing all the necessary supporting programs to encourage recycling. In April 1984, the community became the first in the state to implement a comprehensive curbside recycling program. In 1987, the city broke ground for the Athens County Recycling Center. In the autumn of 1988, the first used-tire roundup was held at the Athens County Fairgrounds, and in the spring of 1989 the first "Ultimate Recycling Day" was held to promote the collection of used tires, metal appliances, other scrap metal, car batteries, textiles, used motor oil and antifreeze, and magazines. . . .

To support the program, each household pays $2.50 per month for curbside recycling collection and $5 per month for weekly trash collection of one 30-gallon container of trash or $9.50 per month for two containers. Stickers for extra bags are $1.50 each, and residents are charged $3 each for untagged bags set out for collection.

The result: Between 1997 and 2001, avoided disposal saved the community about $500,000, and the sale of recyclable materials yielded nearly $1 million in revenue, which was used to purchase trashcans for the community. In addition, though students may not have any experience with paying for trash before living on their own in college, the control PAYT gives them over their own trash costs can ultimately save them money. . . .

Most Committed to PAYT: San Francisco, CA

Not only is San Francisco (pop. 776,733) one of the first communities to implement PAYT, but it runs one of the most comprehensive recycling and reuse programs in the nation, has set a goal to eliminate waste entirely, and has taken the proactive step of aiming to reduce its greenhouse gas emissions within the next decade. With so many programs in place to encourage waste reduction and recycling, San Francisco already shows a waste diversion rate of more than 62%.

PAYT has been around so long (since 1932) in San Francisco that no one even calls it PAYT. Nevertheless, it forms the backbone for all of the other progressive waste reduction efforts the city has been implementing, in particular, the city's "Fantastic Three" program for residential and commercial recycling, composting, and trash. Serving single-family homes, apartments, and small businesses, the Fantastic Three program distributes three different-colored bins for separating materials: blue for traditional commingled recyclables (paper, cardboard, bottles, and cans); green for compostable food scraps, yard trimmings, wooden crates, animal bedding, and soiled paper; and black for any remaining refuse.

This program is the first in the nation to collect food scraps at curbside for composting. The San Francisco Department of the Environment's Residential and Special Projects Recycling Coordinator Kevin Drew notes, "Compost collection is resonating with people in a way we hadn't anticipated." Although some people cannot get over what he calls the "ick" factor, the response to the program is overwhelmingly positive. According to Drew, people grasp the concept of collecting food scraps to compost into soil for growing food that's brought back into the city.

NINE

Forced Recycling Programs Do Not Work

Per Bylund

Per Bylund, a PhD candidate in economics at the University of Missouri, Columbia, is the founding editor of a libertarian/radical Web site, Anarchism.net. From 1998 to 2000 Bylund was an elected municipal council member in his native Sweden, where, he argues in the following viewpoint, nationwide mandatory recycling has failed miserably. Citizens do all the work, he says, spending endless hours sorting, resorting, cleaning, and transporting trash. The government has monopolistic control, Bylund argues, adding new regulations, raising rates, reducing pickup schedules, and hiring "spies" to catch people who do not follow instructions. Sure, forced recycling is officially profitable, Bylund maintains: It is easy to claim savings and resource conservation when the government stops providing services and does not count the time and energy 9 million Swedes invest (involuntarily) for free. But under such coercion, people cheat, lose interest in voluntary innovation, and end up resenting instead of endorsing green practices.

As a Swede I get to hear a lot of the myths of how wonderful a country Sweden supposedly is—the "prosperous socialism" it stands for, a role model for the rest of the world.

Per Bylund, "The Recycling Myth," Ludwig von Mises Institute, February 4, 2008. Reproduced by permission.

For instance, quite a few friends from around the world have commended me on Swedish recycling polices and the Swedish government's take on coercive environmentalism.

The way it has been presented to me, Sweden has succeeded with what most other governments at best dream about: creating an efficient and profitable national system for saving the environment through large-scale recycling. And the people are all in on it! Everybody's recycling.

The latter is actually true: everybody *is* recycling. But that is the result of government force, not a voluntary choice. The state's monopolist garbage-collection "service" no longer accepts garbage: they will only collect leftovers and other biodegradables. Any other kind of garbage that accidentally finds its way to your garbage bin can result in a nice little fine (it really isn't that little) and the whole neighborhood could face increased garbage collection rates (i.e., *even larger* increases than usual—they tend to increase annually or biannually anyway).

So what do you do with your waste? Most homes have a number of trash bins for different kinds of trash: batteries in one; biodegradables in one; wood in one; colored glass in one, other glass in another; aluminum in one, other metals in another; newspapers in one, hard paper in another, and paper that doesn't fit these two categories in a third; and plastic of all sorts in another collection of bins. The materials generally have to be cleaned before thrown away—milk cartons with milk in them cannot be recycled just as metal cans cannot have too much of the paper labels left.

The people of Sweden are thus forced to clean their trash before carefully separating different kinds of materials. This is the future, they say, and it is supposedly good for the environment. (What about the economy?)

When Recycling Is Coercive and Complex, People Cheat

But it doesn't end with the extra work at home and the extra space in each and every kitchen occupied by a variety of trash bins. What do you do with the trash that isn't collected? The

'... AND THIS PIT'S FILLED WITH UNUSED RECYCLING COLLECTION BINS'

CartoonStock.com.

garbage collection service (which nowadays doesn't offer collection too often, usually biweekly or monthly, even though the rates mysteriously seem to be much higher than before) only accepts certain types of garbage, generally only biodegradable food leftovers. But do not worry; it is all taken care of.

The authorities have established trash collection centers in most neighborhoods where you get to throw away your trash.

These "centers" offer numerous containers where you can throw away your trash—there is one container dedicated for each and every kind of trash and they are all neatly color-coded to help you find the right one. But this means you better have separated your aluminum from your other metals and your newspapers from your soft and hard papers before you get here. You wouldn't want to throw away dirty milk cartons or unsorted paper, would you?

But it seems people do just that: they cheat if they believe they are better off doing so. So the authorities have responded by making it more difficult to cheat. Their first measure was to redesign all containers so that it is more difficult throwing the "wrong" trash in them. For instance, containers for glass have only small, round holes where you put your bottles, and containers for hard paper and carton materials have only letter-slit shaped holes (you need to flatten all boxes before recycling—that's the law).

Well, that didn't do the trick. People kept on cheating. And the more difficult the authorities made it to cheat, the more difficult it was to get rid of the trash even if you intended to put it in the right place. So people went to these centers and simply put everything next to the containers instead—why bother? The authorities responded by appointing salaried "trash collection center spies" (!) to document who was cheating so that they could be brought to justice. (There have actually been a few court cases where people have been tried for not following recycling laws.) Need I say the attempt to appoint spies didn't work either? After a rather hot-spirited debate in the media, all spying at trash collection centers was abolished.

The Government Does Save Money . . .

But the real question here is not to what degree the authorities are ignorant of what spurs human action. We already have numerous examples of this ignorance being quite huge. The question is: does this recycling structure *work*? The answer is that, from a government point of view, while it can probably be thought of as working, from an environmental point of view, the answer is definitely "no."

The structure works the way all centrally planned structures work: it increases and centralizes power while the attempted (expected) results do not materialize. In this case, the structure works: people do sort their trash in different bins—they have no choice. Also, government garbage collection companies do not have to do as much work while getting paid more than ever before. People are annoyed, but do not really react. . . .

This coercive recycling structure is set up in layers, where the consumer ("producer" of waste) gets to do most of the work of sorting, cleaning, and transporting the trash to collection centers. Government-appointed companies then empty the containers and transport the materials to regional centers where the trash is prepared for recycling. And then everything is transported to centralized recycling plants where the materials are prepared for reuse or burning. Finally what is left of the materials is sold to companies and individuals at subsidized prices so that they can make "environmentally friendly" choices.

What is interesting about this Soviet-style planned recycling is that it is officially profitable. It is supposed to be resource efficient, since recycling of the materials is less energy-consuming than, for instance, mining or the production of paper from wood. It is also economically profitable, since the government actually generates revenues from selling recycled materials and products made in the recycling process. The final recycling process costs less than is earned from selling the recycled products.

. . . But the Costs to Consumers Far Exceed Recycling Benefits

However, this is common *government* logic: it is "energy saving" simply because government does not count the time and energy used by *nine million people* cleaning and sorting their trash. Government authorities and researchers have reached the conclusion that the cost of (a) the water and electricity used for cleaning household trash, (b) transportation from trash collection centers, and (c) the final recycling process is actually less than would be necessary to produce these materials from scratch. Of

Many Swedish people think that their government's garbage collection service is too restrictive and hurts the economy.

course, they don't count the literally millions of times people drive to the recycling centers to empty their trash bins; neither do they count, for instance, energy and costs for the extra housing space required for a dozen extra trash bins in every home.

Economically, Swedish recycling is a disaster. Imagine a whole population spending time and money cleaning their garbage and driving it around the neighborhood rather than working or investing in a productive market! According to the government's books, more money flows in than flows out; therefore recycling is profitable. But this ignores the costs of coercion.

The government bookkeepers also take advantage of the cost cuts they have been able to realize through centralizing the garbage collection system. These "cuts," however, are mostly cuts in service, whereas rates for consumers have been increased. A recent problem with the garbage-collection centers is that the containers aren't emptied very often (a typical example of government "savings") and thus remain full, which means that people's garbage piles up next to the overflowing containers while the government contractors sit idle: they are only paid to empty the containers on schedule, not to pick up the trash sitting next to these containers. The result? Disease and rats. Newspapers have been reporting on a "rat invasion" in Stockholm and in other Swedish cities in recent years.

If we consider the costs in monetary terms, in terms of wasted time, and in terms of increased emissions from automobiles, this is hardly environmentally friendly. Adding the annoyance and the increased risk for disease, Swedish recycling is at least as disastrous as any other government scheme.

Forced Recycling Discourages Personal and Industry Initiative

This should be expected, since the system is so authoritarian in style, structure, and management. It might be more "high-tech" and advanced than the Soviet systems ever were, but it is still a system founded on command rather than voluntary choice based on interest or incentive. Interestingly enough, the system is too socialist even for Sweden's number one socialist newspaper, *Aftonbladet*. In an op-ed on January 4, 2002, Lena Askling wrote on the public garbage collection system:

> We [consumers] are supposed to sort, compost, parcel, store, and transport the trash. We are supposed to keep on with this cockamamie of storing compost garbage in small containers in apartments and villas and then transport the stinking, leaking trash to dedicated bins or collection centers, which seem to always be brim-full.
>
> Why in the name of the Lord cannot the government introduce "market incentives" to stimulate industry and producers to develop rational packaging and garbage disposal systems enabling recycling, energy production and

future import revenue? And perhaps a consumer friendly and hygienically acceptable system instead of the current trash and filth chaos?

While I'm waiting, mice are scurrying around in my garbage compartment.

Even Askling, who writes socialist propaganda for a living, knows the Swedish recycling scheme doesn't work; and she concludes it is in need of *more market*.

Please enlighten me, wherein lies the so-often-acclaimed *success* of this system?

Bottle Bills Are a Great Incentive to Recycle

Jenny Gitlitz and Pat Franklin

> Passing a national bottle bill that would add a refundable
> deposit to every beverage container at the time of sale is
> the best way to reduce landfill waste, litter, and green-
> house gases; conserve energy and resources; and increase
> recycling rates, Jenny Gitlitz and Pat Franklin argue in
> the following viewpoint. Eleven states already have bottle
> bills, with strong public support, the authors claim, but
> deposit amounts and container categories vary from state
> to state. The authors recommend a ten-cent deposit for
> containers of all beverages, alcoholic or not, carbonated
> or not. That is high enough to make redemption worth-
> while and would, they estimate, bring redemption rates up
> to 95 percent. Gitlitz is research director of the Container
> Recycling Institute, a Connecticut-based nonprofit orga-
> nization that campaigns to make beverage consumption
> sustainable and bring beverage container waste to zero
> by 2020. Bottle-bill expert Franklin is retired executive
> director of the institute, which she founded in 1991.

For over a century, bottlers operated a voluntary deposit-return
system: a mainstay of the American cultural landscape. The
introduction of disposable bottles and cans and the centralization

Jenny Gitlitz and Pat Franklin, *The 10-Cent Incentive to Recycle*. Glastonbury, CT: Container
Recycling Institute, 2006. © 2006, Container Recycling Institute. Reproduced by permission.

of the beverage industry in the 1950's effectively killed the refill-able bottle. Disposable packaging ended the period of wartime frugality: changing consumer habits permanently, and causing container litter to mushroom across the physical landscape.

In response to the growing litter problem, activists and policy-makers fought to secure mandatory deposits on throwaway con-tainers. In 1971, Oregon enacted the nation's first law placing a mandatory, refundable 5¢ deposit on all beer and soda cans and bottles. Vermont followed suit the following year. In effect, this legislation codified the older, voluntary deposit, which for years had functioned well as an incentive to recycle and a disincen-tive to litter. Encouraged by the results, advocates in dozens of other states campaigned for deposit laws, and by 1986, "bottle bills" were in place in 10 states. Several states have updated their deposit laws to include wine, liquor and/or non-carbonated bev-erages. Three decades after Oregon and Vermont made history, their deposit systems are still going strong.

The Public Supports Bottle Deposits

Recent statewide surveys in Michigan, Iowa, and New York found that the public overwhelmingly supports existing bottle bills by a 3 to 1 margin, and they support updating them to include non-carbonated beverages. No state bottle bill has ever been repealed. Nevertheless, the powerful beverage industry lobby has kept all but a handful of new and updated bottle bill proposals "bottled up" in legislative committees.

Bottle bills are popular because they are effective at reducing litter in urban, rural, and recreational areas; keeping trash out of landfills and incinerators; raising funds for community groups; and saving energy and resources—and reducing pollution—on a global level.

Redemption rates for deposit containers range from 65% to 95%, depending on the deposit value. CRI [Container Recycling Institute] estimates that the recycling rates in bottle bill states, which include containers picked up at curbside, are 5–15% higher still. In contrast, beverage container recycling rates in non-deposit states average 30%.

The environmental benefits of these high recycling rates are pronounced. In Michigan alone, an estimated 88 billion aluminum cans and glass and plastic bottles have been recycled through the bottle bill since 1979, saving the energy equivalent of almost 40 million barrels of crude oil and reducing greenhouse gas emissions by about 4.8 million tons. From Oregon to New York, bottle bills have also cut beverage container litter by 70% to 85%, and lowered overall litter by 30% to 65%. In 2002, Hawaii became the 11th state to pass a bottle bill. Legislators voted for deposits not only to stimulate recycling, but as a way to keep Hawaii's beaches cleaner, and to create jobs.

Deposit systems also reduce the tax burden. As elected officials across the country are forced to cut essential programs for schools, veterans, and seniors, public recycling is receiving short shrift. Local officials are re-evaluating the "necessity" of curbside programs and other municipal waste reduction measures. In this budget climate, deposit states are at a distinct advantage: the infrastructure for recycling billions of discarded containers is financed by the producers and consumers of the beverages, not the taxpayers. In recent years, policymakers and activists in most of the deposit states have tried to capitalize on this advantage by working to add non-carbonated drinks to their existing bottle bills.

While municipal curbside recycling programs tripled nationally during the 1990's, they have been unable to keep up with increasing sales of single-serving beverages and away-from-home consumption of food and drinks. About 130 billion beverage bottles and cans were landfilled, littered or incinerated in 2004—twice the number wasted in 1990. Now that cities can no longer afford to pick up the tab, the economic and environmental roles played by deposits are more important than ever. . . .

What Is a Bottle Bill?

A bottle bill is a law that requires a minimum refundable deposit on beer, soda, and other beverage containers. The financial incentive provided by the refundable deposit ensures high beverage

The eleven states with bottle deposit laws have experienced a threefold rise in bottle recycling.

recycling rates, and dramatically reduces container litter. Putting a refundable deposit on beverage containers is not a new idea. The deposit-refund system was created by the beverage industry many decades ago as a means of guaranteeing the return of their glass bottles to be washed, refilled, and re-sold.

Eleven U.S. states have existing laws that require refundable deposits on all beer and carbonated soft drink containers: California, Connecticut, Delaware, Hawaii, Iowa, Maine, Massachusetts, Michigan, New York, Oregon, and Vermont. The laws vary from state to state. Hawaii's and California's laws also cover non-carbonated, non-alcoholic beverages. Maine's law covers all beverage types except dairy and cider drinks. Several states cover wine and/or liquor bottles. Delaware's deposit law exempts aluminum cans.

When a retailer buys packaged beverages from a distributor, a deposit is paid to the distributor for each can or bottle purchased. The consumer pays the deposit to the retailer when buying the beverage. When the consumer returns the empty beverage container to the retail store, to a redemption center, or to a reverse vending machine, the deposit is refunded. The retailer recoups the deposit from the distributor, plus an additional handling fee in most states. The handling fee, which generally ranges from 1–3 cents, helps cover the cost of handling the containers. . . .

Evidence That Bottle Bills Work

The eleven states with deposit systems have consistently achieved beverage container redemption rates two to three times higher than the rates in non–bottle bill states. While the beverage container *redemption* rate averages 70% in the bottle bill states, the actual *recycling* rate is higher (between 75% and 85%), because some consumers choose to recycle their deposit containers through curbside or drop-off programs rather than at the grocery store or redemption center.

The Container Recycling Institute has estimated a national beverage container recycling rate of about 33%, a rate that would be much lower if it were not for the high recycling rates in the eleven deposit states pulling up the national average.

Other data corroborate the higher recycling rates in deposit states. A 2002 multi-stakeholder report by Businesses and Environmentalists Allied for Recycling (BEAR) estimated that the overall U.S. beverage container recycling rate was 40.5% in 1999, and that the average rate in non-deposit states was 28% that year.

The 10¢ Incentive

With a higher financial incentive, the average 70% redemption rate can easily be exceeded. . . . Michigan has a redemption rate of 95%, due to its 10¢ refund value: the only one in the United States. This redemption rate is well above the rates achieved in New York, Massachusetts, Oregon, and Hawaii, where the deposit

Recycling Rates Go Up in Container-Deposit States

	Total Annual Recovery (billions of units)	Per Capita Recovery (units)	Percent of Total U.S. Annual Recovery	Cents per Unit (a)
40 Nondeposit States (71% of U.S. Population)	38.2	191	49%	1.25
10 Deposit States* (29% of U.S. Population)	40.0	490	51%	1.53

(a) Includes revenues from material sales, does not include the forfeited deposit value of unredeemed containers

* As of 2008, 11 states have deposit laws in effect: CA, CT, DE, HI, IA, ME, MA, MI, NY, OR, VT.

Taken from: Container Recycling Institute, "Container Recycling Scoreboard 2007," from Table ES-1, "Understanding Beverage Container Recycling: A Value Chain Assessment Prepared for the Multi-stakeholder Recovery Project," Business and Environmentalists Allied for Recycling (BEAR), 2002.

is 5¢, and in California, where until 2004, the deposit for most containers was only 2.5¢.

Other countries with higher deposit values also achieve higher recycling rates. For example, the voluntary, industry-operated deposit system in Sweden has a deposit value of 50 öre, about 10¢, and has achieved a nationwide aluminum can recycling rate of 85%—forty percentage points higher than the 2004 U.S. aluminum can recycling rate of 45%. Sweden's PET bottle recycling rate was 79.8% in 2004—four times higher than the 21.5% of PET beverage bottles recycled in the U.S. that year.

A nationwide system of 10¢ deposits on beverage containers would virtually guarantee that 80% to 90% of the beverage cans and bottles sold in the United States would be recycled.

ELEVEN

Bottle Bills Are a Poor Incentive to Recycle

Business Wire

> Beware of bottle bills, Business Wire warns voters in the following viewpoint. California's beverage container recycling rate suffered an alarming decline in 2000 as more than 6 billion containers were thrown away instead of recycled, despite a new bottle bill. Bottle bills do not always increase recycling, because people are always on the go and bottle bills leave recycling up to the consumer. The small deposit people receive in return is not enough incentive for people to recycle. Business Wire, a wholly owned subsidiary of Berkshire Hathaway, is the global market leader in commercial news distribution.

California's beverage container recycling rate suffered an alarming decline in 2000 to 61 percent as more than six billion containers were thrown away instead of recycled, according to figures released today [May 24, 2001] by the California Department of Conservation.

Bottle Bills Don't Always Increase Recycling

To stop the drop in recycling, the department is launching a campaign to motivate Californians to recycle more.

"Dramatic Drop in Beverage Container Recycling Rate Sparks Concern by Department of Conservation Officials," Business Wire, May 24, 2001, p. 252.

"Recycling is one of those things where more is always better," said Darryl Young, California Department of Conservation director. "Californians can do more."

The trashed aluminum, glass and plastic represents an estimated $158 million in unredeemed California Refund Value (CRV) deposits. Laid end-to-end, the unrecycled beverage containers would circle the earth nearly seven times.

The total number of recycled containers, 10.2 billion in 2000, has remained fairly stable for the past 10 years. However, last year's new bottle bill added some 3.4 billion containers to the program. A decline in the recycling rate was not wholly unexpected, but the size of the drop—from 74 percent to 61 percent—came as a surprise.

"We expected a drop, but not like this," said Young. "We're Californians, we're supposed to know more about recycling."

The average recycling rate during the 1990s was 77 percent. The addition of new CRV containers—many of them plastic, which historically has been recycled at lower rates than aluminum—is cited by the department as a primary reason for the decline.

Young also pointed to the on-the-go lifestyle of many Californians as a factor. According to recent focus group research conducted by the department, Californians are more mobile than ever and less likely to recycle while away from home. Additionally, consumer beverage consumption in recent years has grown to include bottled water and sports drinks, generally marketed in plastic containers.

"Many people don't realize a plastic beverage container is redeemed for the same value as an aluminum or glass container," Young said.

New Recycling Campaign

The campaign—which utilizes television, print and radio advertisements, as well as billboards and an Internet site (www. bottlesandcans.com)—is designed to motivate Californians to recycle more.

In 2000, in response to California's startling drop in its beverage container recycling rate, the state's Department of Conservation searched for ways to motivate consumers to recycle.

The theme for the campaign is "Recycle. It's good for the bottle. It's good for the can."

"We need to do more than raise awareness in the minds of Californians, we need to change behavior," Young said. "That's why the outreach campaign is so important."

California is one of 10 states with a beverage container recycling program. The Department of Conservation administers the

California Beverage Container Recycling and Litter Reduction Act, which became law in 1986. The primary goal of the act is to achieve and maintain high recycling rates for each beverage container type included in the program.

Consumers pay CRV (California Refund Value) when they purchase beverages from a retailer. The deposits are refunded when empty containers are redeemed through local recycling centers. More information on the state's beverage container recycling program is available at www.bottlesandcans.com or by calling 1-800-RECYCLE.

In addition to promotion of the state's beverage container recycling program, the Department of Conservation administers programs to safeguard agricultural and open-space land; regulates oil, gas and geothermal wells in the state; studies and maps earthquakes, landslides and mineral resources; and ensures reclamation of land used for mining.

TWELVE

Plastic Bags Are Better than Paper

Skaidra Smith-Heisters

In the decades-long paper-versus-plastic debate, environ-mentalists long claimed that paper bags are better because unlike plastic, paper is 100 percent biodegradable, 100 percent recyclable, and produced from a renewable natural resource, wood. In 1990, however, a landmark study by researchers Franklin Associates gave the edge to plastic bags, concluding that plastic consumes less total energy, takes up much less landfill space, and produces much less atmospheric pollution. In the following viewpoint Skaidra Smith-Heisters agrees that plastic is less harmful to the environment, applauds the rising recycling rate for plastic (which doubled from 2005 to 2006), and criticizes retailers such as Whole Foods that are banning plastic bags. That is only going to drive more shoppers to paper, she contends, and reinforce their mistaken perception that paper is the responsible choice. Skaidra Smith-Heisters is a policy analyst at Reason Foundation, a libertarian think tank and publisher headquartered in Los Angeles.

Whole Foods Market won't offer plastic shopping bags at their stores after Earth Day [2008]. It is a savvy move for the upscale natural foods retailer, who estimates that by the

Skaidra Smith-Heisters, "Paper Bags Require More Energy than Plastic Bags," Reason Foundation, April 17, 2008. Reproduced by permission.

end of the year the policy will have averted use of 100 million new plastic grocery bags at their 270 stores. It won't save the company any money—since the paper and multi-use bags that will replace plastic bags at their stores cost more to manufacture, stock and handle—but it is a savvy public relations move that will likely help to soothe the guilty environmental consciences of devoted Whole Foods shoppers who, like most Americans, believe paper bags are environmentally superior to plastic bags.

Unfortunately, the reality is that paper isn't better than plastic.

Paper Bags Consume Five Times More Energy than Plastic

One hundred million new plastic grocery bags require the total energy equivalent of approximately 8300 barrels of oil for extraction of the raw materials, through manufacturing, transport, use and curbside collection of the bags. Of that, 30 percent is oil and 23 percent is natural gas actually used in the bag—the rest is fuel used along the way. That sounds like a lot until you consider that the same number of paper grocery bags use five times that much total energy. A paper grocery bag isn't just made out of trees. Manufacturing 100 million paper bags with one-third post-consumer recycled content requires petroleum energy inputs equivalent to approximately 15,100 barrels of oil plus additional inputs from other energy sources including hydroelectric power, nuclear energy and wood waste.

Making sound environmental choices is hard, especially when the product is "free," like bags at most grocery stores. When the cashier rings up a purchase and bags it in a paper bag, the consumer doesn't see that it took at least a gallon of water to produce that bag (more than 20 times the amount used to make a plastic bag), that it weighed 10 times more on the delivery truck and took up seven times as much space as a plastic bag in transit to the store, and will ultimately result in between tens and hundreds of times more greenhouse gas emissions than a plastic bag.

Proponents of plastic over paper bags say that paper bags require five times the amount of energy to produce as plastic bags.

Biodegradable bags don't fare much better than paper bags; in a recent life cycle analysis, one type of compostable plastic bag was found to use somewhat less total energy and generate less solid waste, but represent more fossil fuel use, greenhouse gas emissions, and fresh water use than the comparable paper bag.

Part of the invisible cost of shopping bags is passed down to consumers as retailers recoup the price they pay for the bags—pennies in the case of plastic, a nickel or a dime for paper bags (ones with handles cost more), and the same or more again for biodegradable plastic bags. Costs like greenhouse gas emissions and air or water pollution might eventually be captured in a carbon tax, cap-and-trade scheme, or regulatory fee (again, ultimately passed down to consumers, whether they are aware of it or not). Still other costs are borne by the public (e.g. litter pick-up) or in less calculable ways (e.g. diminished aesthetic values or impacts to marine animals).

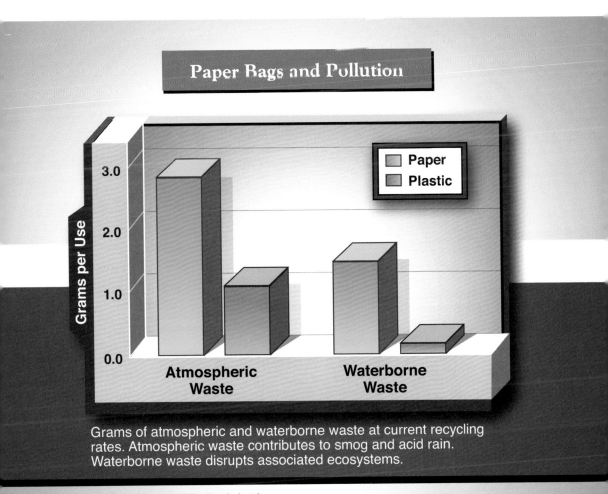

Grams of atmospheric and waterborne waste at current recycling rates. Atmospheric waste contributes to smog and acid rain. Waterborne waste disrupts associated ecosystems.

All figures courtesy of Roplast Industries.

Taken from: Plastic Bag Economics.com, "Paper Vs. Plastic," *Plastic Bags: Friend or Foe?*

More People Reuse Plastic Bags

The good news is that, given a choice between plastic, paper and multi-use grocery bags, most people make the best available environmental choice: whichever bag they are most likely to reuse. In an informal online MSNBC survey last month [April 2008], 38 percent of respondents said reusability was the most important factor in choosing what type of grocery bag to use. The plurality, 41 percent, choose plastic. Twenty-eight percent reported that environmental concerns were their top consideration and—unfortunately, given the comparative life cycle analyses—56 percent believed that paper is more "environmentally friendly."

The vast majority of people reuse "single-use" plastic bags for household tasks like bagging garbage and cleaning up messes. Ireland's plastic bag tax, initiated in 2002 to combat the aesthetic impacts of litter on tourism, virtually eliminated the use of the targeted bags but also resulted in a 77 percent increase in the sale of kitchen garbage bags. San Francisco's first-in-the-nation ban on non-biodegradable plastic bags last year [2007] surely has had similar rebound effects.

Nationwide, the most recent Environmental Protection Agency data show recycling rates for broad categories that include paper and plastic grocery bags to be 25 and 9 percent, respectively. The recycling rate for plastic is growing quickly under the pressure of new mandates and markets. The actual amount recovered nationwide doubled between 2005 and 2006. Most of the plastic bags recycled are reclaimed for use in the United States or Canada to manufacture decking, railing and fencing which replace the use of virgin forest products.

Plastic Takes Up Less Landfill Space

For those bags that aren't recycled, misconceptions about plastic and paper bags follow them all the way to their graves. In a landfill, paper bags, petroleum-based plastic bags and even degradable plastic bags share roughly the same fate. Modern landfills are managed for stability, not decomposition. Plastic bags can be better in a landfill because their compact size takes up the least space and, as opposed to biodegradable bags, they release zero greenhouse gas emissions.

Reusable shopping bags may be the norm at Whole Foods a year from now, but they're not for everyone in every circumstance. A multi-use plastic or durable bag is environmentally and economically cost-effective only if it is actually used multiple times. Some of these bags are recyclable or compostable, others are not. The basic principles of conservation apply here: the greenest individual choice is the one that results in the greatest actual reduction, reuse and recycling.

Less than a year after a law requiring grocery stores to accept plastic bags for recycling took effect, lawmakers in California are now proposing mandatory reductions in plastic bag use and up to a 25-cent charge for plastic grocery bags statewide.

Those who are cognizant of the environmental realities of the paper versus plastic debate, but nevertheless believe providing complimentary plastic bags at grocery stores should be illegal, cling optimistically to the idea that plastic grocery bags can be erased from the environmental equation without unintended consequences. At present, the only honest assessment is that a plastic bag ban is a de facto paper bag mandate, and increased use of paper bags means an increase in environmental ills including air and water pollution, greater energy and water use and higher greenhouse gas emissions.

In a sense, the persistent view of plastic bag use as emblematic of the nation's progress on environmental issues is right for the wrong reasons. It shows how far good intentions coupled with bad information can lead us astray.

THIRTEEN

Plastic Bags Are a Recycling Nightmare

Katharine Mieszkowski

In the following viewpoint, American journalist Katharine
Mieszkowski disputes the idea that recycling rates and
methods for plastic are improving and using plastic is okay
because it is less harmful to the environment than paper
anyway. On the contrary, Mieszkowski argues, only 2 percent of the 100 billion plastic bags that Americans throw
away each year are recycled. That figure is not likely to
get higher soon; even advanced recycling centers "simply
cannot master the plastic bag," which clogs machinery.
What *is* recycled is not true recycling, according to the
author; plastic bags cannot be recycled into new plastic
bags, only composite decking and a few other products
that themselves cannot be recycled and, like the rest of
the world's plastic debris, will never degrade. Mieszkowski
covers technology and the environment for the Internet
magazine *Salon*, for which she has been a senior writer
since 2000.

The plastic bag is an icon of convenience culture, by some
estimates the single most ubiquitous consumer item on Earth,
numbering in the trillions. They're made from petroleum or natural gas with all the attendant environmental impacts of harvesting

Katharine Mieszkowski, "Plastic Bags Are Killing Us," *Salon*, August 10, 2007. This article first
appeared in *Salon*, at www.salon.com. An online version remains in the *Salon* archives. Reprinted
with permission.

fossil fuels. One recent study found that the inks and colorants used on some bags contain lead, a toxin. Every year, Americans throw away some 100 billion plastic bags after they've been used to transport a prescription home from the drugstore or a quart of milk from the grocery store. It's equivalent to dumping nearly 12 million barrels of oil.

1 Percent Recycled, 99 Percent Garbage Forever

Only 1 percent of plastic bags are recycled worldwide—about 2 percent in the U.S.—and the rest, when discarded, can persist for centuries. They can spend eternity in landfills, but that's not always the case. "They're so aerodynamic that even when they're properly disposed of in a trash can they can still blow away and become litter," says Mark Murray, executive director of Californians Against Waste. It's as litter that plastic bags have the most baleful effect. And we're not talking about your everyday eyesore.

Once aloft, stray bags cartwheel down city streets, alight in trees, billow from fences like flags, clog storm drains, wash into rivers and bays and even end up in the ocean, washed out to sea. Bits of plastic bags have been found in the nests of albatrosses in the remote Midway Islands. Floating bags can look all too much like tasty jellyfish to hungry marine critters. According to the Blue Ocean Society for Marine Conservation, more than a million birds and 100,000 marine mammals and sea turtles die every year from eating or getting entangled in plastic. The conservation group estimates that 50 percent of all marine litter is some form of plastic. There are 46,000 pieces of plastic litter floating in every square mile of ocean, according to the United Nations Environment Programme. In the Northern Pacific Gyre, a great vortex of ocean currents, there's now a swirling mass of plastic trash about 1,000 miles off the coast of California, which spans an area that's twice the size of Texas, including fragments of plastic bags. There's six times as much plastic as biomass, including plankton and jellyfish, in the gyre. "It's an endless stream of incessant plastic particles everywhere you look," says Dr. Marcus

Only a Tiny Amount of Plastic Waste Is Recycled

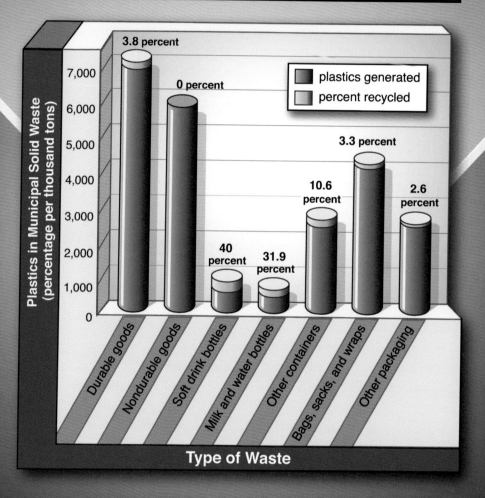

Plastics in Municipal Solid Waste (percentage per thousand tons)

- plastics generated
- percent recycled

3.8 percent

0 percent

3.3 percent

10.6 percent

2.6 percent

40 percent

31.9 percent

Durable goods

Nondurable goods

Soft drink bottles

Milk and water bottles

Other containers

Bags, sacks, and wraps

Other packaging

Type of Waste

Taken from: U.S. Environmental Protection Agency, "Recycling the Hard Stuff," July 2002.

Eriksen, director of education and research for the Algalita Marine Research Foundation, which studies plastics in the marine environment. "Fifty or 60 years ago, there was no plastic out there."

Following the lead of countries like Ireland, Bangladesh, South Africa, Thailand and Taiwan, some U.S. cities are striking back against what they see as an expensive, wasteful and unnecessary mess. [In 2007] San Francisco and Oakland outlawed the use of plastic bags in large grocery stores and pharmacies, permitting only paper bags with at least 40 percent recycled content or otherwise compostable bags. . . . Already the city of Oakland is being sued by an association of plastic bag manufacturers calling itself the Coalition to Support Plastic Bag Recycling. Meanwhile, other communities across the country, including Santa Monica, Calif., New Haven, Conn., Annapolis, Md., and Portland, Ore., are considering taking drastic legislative action against the bags. In Ireland, a now 22-cent tax on plastic bags has slashed their use by more than 90 percent since 2002. In flood-prone Bangladesh, where plastic bags choked drainage systems, the bags have been banned since 2002.

The problem with plastic bags isn't just where they end up, it's that they never seem to end. "All the plastic that has been made is still around in smaller and smaller pieces," says Stephanie Barger, executive director of the Earth Resource Foundation, which has undertaken a Campaign Against the Plastic Plague. Plastic doesn't biodegrade. That means unless they've been incinerated—a noxious proposition—every plastic bag you've ever used in your entire life, including all those bags that the newspaper arrives in on your doorstep, even on cloudless days when there isn't a sliver of a chance of rain, still exists in some form, even fragmented bits, and will exist long after you're dead.

Recycling Facilities Cannot Process Plastic Bags

Grand efforts are under way to recycle plastic bags, but so far those efforts have resulted mostly in a mass of confusion. A tour of Recycle Central in San Francisco makes it easy to see why. The plant is a Willie Wonka factory of refuse. Located on a bay pier with a stunning view of the downtown skyline, some 700 tons of discarded annual reports, Rolling Rock bottles, Diet Coke cans, Amazon.com cardboard boxes, Tide plastic detergent bottles and StarKist tuna fish cans surge into this warehouse every weekday, dumped from trucks into a great clattering, shifting mound. The building tinkles and thumps with the sound of thousands of pounds of glass, aluminum, paper, plastic and cardboard knocking together, as all this detritus passes through a dizzying network of conveyor belts, spinning disks, magnets and gloved human hands to emerge as 16 different sorted, recyclable commodities, baled up by the ton to be shipped or trucked away and made into something new again. It's one way that the city of San Francisco manages to divert some 69 percent of its waste from landfills. But this city's vaunted recycling program, which is so advanced that it can collect coffee grounds and banana peels from urbanites' apartment kitchens and transform them into compost used to grow grapes in Napa Valley vineyards, simply cannot master the plastic bag.

Ask John Jurinek, the plant manager at Recycle Central, what's wrong with plastic bags and he has a one-word answer: "Everything." Plastic bags, of which San Franciscans use some 180 million per year, cannot be recycled here. Yet the hopeful arrow symbol emblazoned on the bags no doubt inspires lots of residents to toss their used ones into the blue recycling bin, feeling good that they've done the right thing. But that symbol on all kinds of plastic items by no means guarantees they can be recycled curbside. (The plastic bags collected at the recycling plant are trucked to the regular dump.) By chucking their plastic bags in the recycling, what those well-meaning San Franciscans have done is throw a plastic wrench into the city's grand recycling factory. If you want to recycle a plastic bag it's better to bring it back to the store where you got it.

As the great mass of recyclables moves past the initial sort deck on a series of spinning disks, stray plastic bags clog the machinery. It's such a problem that one machine is shut down while a worker wearing kneepads and armed with a knife spends an hour climbing precariously on the disks to cut the bags out, yielding a Medusa's hair-mass of wrenched and twisted plastic. In the middle of the night, when the vast sorting operation grinds to a halt to prepare for the next 700-ton day, two workers will spend hours at this dirty job.

Some states are attacking the recycling problem by trying to encourage shoppers to take the bags back to grocery stores.

Proponents of paper bags over plastic bags point to the costs and difficulties of recycling plastic bags.

California requires large grocery stores and pharmacies that distribute the bags known in the trade as T-shirt bags—those common polyethylene bags with two handles, usually made from petroleum or natural gas—to take them back for recycling, and to print instructions on the bags to encourage shoppers to return them to the stores. San Francisco Environment Department spokesperson Mark Westlund, who can see plastic bags lodged in the trees on Market Street from his second-story office window, is skeptical about the state's ability to get shoppers to take back their bags. "We've had in store recycling in San Francisco for over 10 years, and it's never really been successful," says Westlund, who estimates that the city achieved only a 1 percent recycling rate of plastic bags at the stores. "People have to pack up the bags, bring them into the store and drop them off. I think you'd be more inclined to bring your own bag than do that."

Recycling Plastic Really Means "Downcycling"

Regardless, polyethylene plastic bags are recyclable, says Howie Fendley, a senior environmental chemist for MBDC, an ecological design firm. "It's a matter of getting the feedstock to the point where a recycler can economically justify taking those bags and recycling them. The problem is they're mostly air. There has to be a system in place where they get a nice big chunk of polyethylene that can be mechanically ground, melted and then re-extruded."

So far that system nationwide consists mainly of supermarkets and superstores like Wal-Mart voluntarily stockpiling the bags brought back in by conscientious shoppers, and selling them to recyclers or plastic brokers, who in turn sell them to recyclers. In the U.S., one company buys half of the used plastic bags available on the open market in the United States, using about 1.5 billion plastic bags per year. That's Trex, based in Winchester, Va., which makes composite decking out of the bags and recycled wood. It takes some 2,250 plastic bags to make a single 16-foot-long, 2-inch-by-6-inch plank. It might feel good to buy decking made out of something that otherwise could have choked a sea turtle, but not so fast. That use is not an example of true recycling, points out Carol Misseldine, sustainability coordinator for the city of Oakland. "We're not recycling plastic bags into plastic bags," she says. "They're being downcycled, meaning that they're being put into another product that itself can never be recycled."

Unlike a glass beer bottle or an aluminum can, it's unusual that a plastic bag is made back into another plastic bag, because it's typically more expensive than just making a new plastic bag. After all, the major appeal of plastic bags to stores is that they're much cheaper than paper. Plastic bags cost grocery stores under 2 cents per bag, while paper goes for 4 to 6 cents and compostable bags 9 to 14 cents. However, says Eriksen from the Algalita Marine Research Foundation, "The long-term cost of having these plastic bags blowing across our landscape, across our beaches and accumulating in the northern Pacific far outweighs the short-term loss to a few."

Of course, shoppers could just bring their own canvas bags, and avoid the debate altogether. The California bag recycling law also requires stores to sell reusable bags. Yet it will be a sad irony if outlawing the bags, as San Francisco and Oakland have, doesn't inspire shoppers to bring their own canvas bags, but simply sends them to paper bags, which come with their own environmental baggage. In fact, plastic bags were once thought to be an ecologically friendly alternative to cutting down trees to make paper ones. It takes 14 million trees to produce the 10 billion paper grocery bags used every year by Americans, according to the Natural Resource Defense Council. Yet suggesting that plastic bags made out of petroleum are a better choice burns up Barger from the Earth Resources Foundation. "People say, 'I'm using plastic. I'm saving trees,'" she says. "But have you ever seen what Shell, Mobil and Chevron are doing down in the rain forests to get oil?"

Use Recycled Paper, or Better Yet, Canvas

Gordon Bennett, an executive in the San Francisco Bay chapter of the Sierra Club, agrees. "The fundamental thing about trees is that if you manage them properly they're a renewable resource," he says. "I haven't heard about the oil guys growing more oil lately." Still, as the plastic bag industry never tires of pointing out, paper bags are heavier than plastic bags, so they take more fossil fuels to transport. Some life cycle assessments have put plastic bags out ahead of paper, when it comes to energy and waste in the manufacturing process. But paper bags with recycled content, like those soon to be required in San Francisco and Oakland, use less energy and produce less waste than those made from virgin paper.

The only salient answer to paper or plastic is neither. Bring a reusable canvas bag, says Darby Hoover, a senior resource specialist for the Natural Resources Defense Council. However, if you have to make a choice between the two, she recommends taking whichever bag you're more likely to reuse the most times, since, like many products, the production of plastic or paper bags has the biggest environmental impact, not the disposal of them. "Reusing is a better option because it avoids the purchase of another product."

Some stores, like IKEA, have started trying to get customers to bring their own bags by charging them 5 cents per plastic bag. The Swedish furniture company donates the proceeds from the bag sales to a conservation group. Another solution just might be fashion. Bringing your own bag—or BYOB as Whole Foods dubs it—is the latest eco-chic statement. When designer Anya Hindmarch's "I am not a plastic bag" bag hit stores in Taiwan, there was so much demand for the limited-edition bag that the riot police had to be called in to control a stampede, which sent 30 people to the hospital.

FOURTEEN

Reducing and Reusing Is Better than Recycling

Melissa M. Ezarik

> Melissa M. Ezarik is managing editor at Professional Media Group in Norwalk, Connecticut, publisher of education-related magazines *University Business* and *District Administration*. In the following viewpoint, Ezarik argues that in the effort to reduce waste and protect the environment, reuse is more important, and much more effective, than recycling. Everything that is recycled consumes energy in manufacture and more energy in disposal or reprocessing, she maintains, while reusing items instead of tossing and replacing is true source reduction. Ezarik recommends four reuse practices: Reuse an item yourself for original or new purposes. If you cannot, give it to someone who can. Alternatively, resell it to recoup the cost and prolong its useful life. And buy used, to extend the life of an item and save money.

We're a society filled with environmental do-gooders. Most of us have picked up the habit of collecting piles of newspapers and lugging them out to the curb and filling our blue recycling bins with plastics and glass.

Some of us go the extra green mile, always on the lookout for recycling drives and even paying to have old household appliances

Melissa M. Ezarik, "2007 Living Green, Saving Green Guide: Recycling's Great—Reusing Is Better," www.bankrate.com, October 4, 2007. Reproduced by permission.

Four Ways to Reuse

Once an item is no longer new, there are several ways to either make money or save money.	
Reuse it . . .	for its original purpose or a new purpose.
Give it away . . .	to someone who can reuse it.
Sell it . . .	to recoup original cost while reusing.
Buy it used . . .	reuse it and save money.

Taken from: Melissa M. Ezarik, "2007 Living Green, Saving Green Guide: Recycling's Great—Reusing Is Beter," Bankrate.com, October 4, 2007. Reproduced by permission.

and technology recycled. Buying natural and organic items for our homes is a source of pride, as well. We are doing our part to save the planet, and we're proud of it.

But the second of the "three R'S"—reduce, reuse, recycle— doesn't seem to be getting its fair share of the action.

The Image Problem: Recycling Saves the Planet, Reusing Is Just Cheap

"Keeping up with the Joneses can influence how people want to be perceived. Recycling can be a good duty, while reusing is being cheap and maybe indicating that you don't have enough finances to buy new," says Donna Watkins, whose Web site TheFrugalLife. com and 13,400-circulation e-mail newsletter provide information on how to live frugally with the resources you have.

Recycling—breaking down items into raw materials to be used again—is important, but environmental experts know reusing is more important, notes Jim Mihelcic, a professor of civil and environmental engineering at Michigan Technological University and past codirector of the institution's Sustainable Futures Institute.

Unfortunately, Mihelcic adds, most people see it the other way around. "Recycling is much cooler than reusing," Mihelcic says. "It's a more visual thing to do. It's an easy way for people to connect with environmental issues. Reuse is kind of lost."

Besides the "cheap" perception, the belief that it's too time-consuming also keeps people from reusing, Watkins says. "Although it saves time by reusing what you already have in the home, it takes a new lifestyle choice to organize the stuff you have and look around for an answer to your need before going shopping." Reusing comes most easily to those from the Depression era. Baby boomers are buyers. "Advertising has trained us to believe new is better," Watkins adds.

Mark Caserta, a former lobbyist for the New York League of Conservation Voters, can recall his grandmother saying of many items, "Can't we save and reuse it?" and his mother replying, "Why do that when you could just throw it out?"

Now Caserta is co-owner, with his wife, of the Brooklyn store 3r Living, which carries products aimed at reducing waste, reusing unwanted or discarded materials, and recycling. Yet, it's the recycling aspect of the business that gets people's attention most. "When people come to our store, almost universally they call it the recycling store," Caserta says.

Why Reuse?

Waste prevention, also known as source reduction, is a convincing reason to use and reuse products. "Preventing waste saves natural resources and the energy consumed to make new products. It also reduces greenhouse gases associated with manufacturing and waste disposal, and it saves disposal costs," reminds Roxanne Smith, a press officer for the U.S. Environmental Protection Agency [EPA].

Lynda Grose, an adjunct professor of sustainable fashion design at the California College of the Arts and a consultant on sustainable design issues for Gap and other companies, puts it like this: "There's no such thing as disposable. Everything goes somewhere." Not to mention, there are environmental stresses with each stage of the product life cycle, from pre-manufacturing and manufacturing to packaging and transport, she adds.

Between 2 percent and 5 percent of the waste stream is potentially reusable, according to the EPA. While reuse can mean keeping something with the same owner—for its original or a new use—it can also mean redistributing materials to those who would find a use for them.

Many experts say that it is better for the environment to use reusable cloth bags over paper and plastic bags.

Any form of reuse can mean saving money. Mihelcic has observed that people get excited about extra money in their pockets when politicians talk about tax breaks, yet don't tend to see reuse as a way of putting money in their pockets. "Reusing actually saves you more than a tax break," he points out.

In more than 6,000 communities nationwide, there's an added economic motivation to reuse: The less you throw away, the less you pay for waste removal. In these "pay-as-you-throw" towns and cities, residents pay for waste removal based on how much waste they produce.

Here's a closer look at the four major reuse practices:

1. Reuse it for its original purpose or a new purpose.

Many everyday items, such as bags and containers, can be used more than once, the EPA reminds.

Purchasing with reuse in mind is important, too. Cloth napkins, cloth diapers, dish cloths, quality tools and appliances, and refillable items all fit the bill. And don't underestimate the environmental impact of discarding broken items either. Can they be repaired and then reused?

As for clothing, practicality rules with reuse. While buying something made of organic fabric may seem the best environmental choice, it's actually not if you wind up wearing the item only once and tossing it, notes Grose. Better to wear every item you buy again and again, repairing as necessary.

Take a yellow retro dress Grose owns that she often wears to weddings. Rather than retire it after she discovered a strawberry stain, she embroidered over the stain the names of the friends married that day.

2. Give it away to someone who can reuse it.

Many household items could easily be used again for another purpose, including empty glass and plastic jars, milk jugs, coffee cans and similar containers for storing leftovers, buttons, nails, etc. Just be sure to keep practical safety in mind, the EPA reminds. Don't reuse containers that originally held products such as motor oil or pesticides, don't store anything potentially harmful in containers designed for food or beverages and always label containers and store them out of reach of children and pets.

Those willing to get creative have a host of other options, as well. Use extra lumber pieces for smaller projects, such as a birdhouse or mailbox.

Clothing could be put to use in many ways. Grose, for instance, made a curtain for her daughter's bedroom out of an old striped shirt she had purchased secondhand back when she was a student. And she took a pair of favorite pajama pants that she'd worn over 20 years ago and made a pillow for her daughter's bed. "There are memories in that pillow. It's not just a Pottery Barn pillow," she says. (Not to mention, it didn't come with a Pottery Barn price.)

"The X and Y generations have been schooled in dozens of do-it-yourself programs and literature to boost creative ways and ideas of how to reuse with style," says Terra Wellington, a wellness lifestyle expert who has spoken on television about environmental tips for families and is currently writing a book on eco-tips for moms. "Don't like the color? Change it. Don't like the shape? Cut it down to size. Don't enjoy an item? Turn it into something else of use."

Creative solutions aren't limited to reuse of tangible items. "Think about how you run your house," says Mihelcic, who converted his own home, an old farmhouse, into an environmentally friendly structure, with solar hot water heating and other green features.

Waste water collected from clothes washers, bathtubs, showers, and laundry or bathroom sinks, for example, is known as gray water and can be safely reused (where not prohibited) for household gardening, composting, and lawn and landscape irrigation. (Advice and tips for using gray water can be found on the Arizona Department of Environmental Quality Web site.)

3. Sell it: recoup original cost while reusing.

Checking in with family and friends may be the easiest way to find a new home for old items, from tools to camera equipment to children's toys. Caserta estimates that 90 percent of the clothing his daughter wears was handed down from people he knows. The networks Freecycle and FreeSharing are two places to find local people in need of specific items.

When looking to simply drop off unwanted items, good options include Goodwill, Red Cross, United Way and the Salvation Army. There are more than 6,000 of these and other "reuse centers" around the country, according to the EPA.

Also consider schools, day care facilities and senior centers as donation spots, especially for items (such as egg cartons and colored paper) that could be used as crafts projects. Computer equipment and other electronics may also be welcome; some agencies that facilitate the donation of used computers can be found at the EPA's Web site.

Keep in mind: Donations to nonprofit reuse operations with 501(c)3 status can result in a tax deduction based on fair market value.

4. Buy it used—reuse it and save money.

Call it practicing reuse for a profit—or "entrepreneurial reuse," as Wellington does. Whether it's through a tag sale, the classifieds or an online auction on eBay, finding a buyer for items you don't want keeps them out of landfills.

Buying one of those items keeps reuse going, too. "It's important to buy at Goodwill as well as drop off at Goodwill," Grose reminds, adding that specialty designers are a source of reused items as well. For example, Used Rubber USA creates bags, wallets and other items out of reclaimed industrial rubber; Crispina rugs, blankets and other products incorporate sweater fabrics; and the Green Glass Company makes drinking glasses out of old bottles.

Just be sure you don't buy what you don't truly need. For Mihelcic, that meant reusing the infrastructure of his old home while refurbishing it, even though it meant constraints on the design. From the manufacture of the original home's tiles to its concrete, "There's a tremendous amount of embodied energy, embodied water that went into creating what went into your house," he says.

When Grose hears people in her industry say things like, "Now all my sheets are organic," she can't help but think, "What happened to your old ones?"

What You Should Know About Recycling

Recycling Is:

- Collecting, separating, processing, and reusing materials, in the same form as the original or in new forms, instead of discarding them as waste.
- Mechanically separating and treating waste to recover reusable material, other than by incineration.
- A closed loop: Collection and sorting of recyclables is only the first step. Producing new products from recycled material is the second step. Purchasing and using recycled-content products closes the loop.

There Are Three Main Types of Recycling:

- Industrial waste recycling involves "pre-consumer waste": the by-products or leftover raw materials, both hazardous and nonhazardous, of large plants such as petroleum refineries, chemical companies, paper mills, automobile manufacturers, and public utilities. Recycling at these facilities often means capturing and reprocessing materials to reuse in a company's own production cycle.
- Municipal solid waste (MSW) recycling involves ordinary household and commercial trash, or "post-consumer" waste: paper, glass, plastic, metals, textiles, furniture, and electronics. MSW also includes household hazardous waste (HHW) such as

paint, cleaners, oils, batteries, and pesticides, and organic waste such as food scraps and yard trimmings.

- Composting is "natural recycling," the biological breakdown of organic MSW—food scraps, leaves and grass clippings, live-stock manure—into soil amendments and mulch.

Facts About Municipal Solid Waste (MSW) Production and Disposal

- In 2006, U.S. residents and businesses produced more than 251 million tons of MSW, or about 4.6 pounds of waste per person per day.
- Currently in the United States, 32.5 percent of MSW is recovered and recycled or composted; 12.5 percent is burned at combustion facilities; and the remaining 55 percent is disposed of in landfills.
- Americans recycle 99 percent of batteries, 52 percent of paper and paperboard, 62 percent of yard trimmings; 31 percent of plastic soft drink bottles; 45 percent of aluminum cans; and 67 percent of major household appliances.
- Americans purchase more than 30 billion water bottles per year; 26 billion end up in landfills.
- The number of landfills in the United States has steadily decreased from 8,000 in 1988 to 1,754 in 2006. New landfills are much larger than in the past, however, so total landfill capacity has remained about the same.
- 75 million Americans subscribe to pay-as-you-throw (PAYT) waste collection programs, which are now in place in 30 of the largest 100 cities. Recycling rates in PAYT communities average 17.1 percent versus 13.6 percent in non-PAYT communities.
- 400 million consumer electronics—TVs, VCRs, DVD players, camcorders, stereo equipment, cell phones, and computers—are scrapped each year in the United States; only 12.5 percent of this e-waste is recycled.
- In February 2009, TV stations will stop broadcasting analog signals and switch to digital signals, instantly consigning mil-

lions of older TVs to the e-waste stream if consumers opt to buy new models instead of set-top converter boxes.

What Can and Cannot Be Recycled

- According to the National Recycling Coalition, the top ten items to recycle are aluminum, PET plastic bottles, newspaper, corrugated cardboard, steel cans, HDPE plastic bottles, glass containers, magazines, mixed paper, and computers.
- Used aluminum beverage cans are the most recycled item in the United States, but aluminum siding, gutters, car parts, storm window frames, pie pans, foil wrap, and lawn furniture can also be recycled an unlimited number of times.
- Motor oil can be recycled and refined an unlimited number of times.
- Glass: Clear, green, and amber jars and bottles can be recycled. Lightbulbs, dishes, Pyrex, and crystal cannot.
- Paper: Newspapers, boxes, egg cartons, phone books, and white office paper can be recycled. Waxed, plastic-coated, or foil-coated paper cannot. Paper that is contaminated with food residue, such as greasy pizza boxes, cannot.
- Plastic: Of the seven resin codes stamped on plastic products, only code 1 (PET, soda and water bottles, medicine containers) and code 2 (HDPE, milk and water bottles, laundry detergent bottles, toys) are widely recyclable. PVC pipe, plastic meat wrap, cooking oil bottles, shrink wrap, plastic grocery bags, syrup bottles, yogurt tubs, diapers, and Styrofoam usually are not accepted at local recycling facilities.
- End uses for recycled PET include: fiberfill, strapping, carpeting, engineering plastics, nonfood bottles. End uses for recycled HDPE include: nonfood bottles, curbside recyclables containers, flower pots, drainage pipes, and boat piers. End uses for recycled commingled or mixed plastic include: plastic lumber, picnic tables, fencing, car stops, and park benches.
- Eleven states have enacted "bottle bills"—laws that impose five-cent or ten-cent refundable deposits on beverage containers—in an effort to reduce litter and increase recycling rates: California,

Connecticut, Delaware, Hawaii, Iowa, Maine, Massachusetts, Michigan (which now boasts a 97.3 percent redemption rate), New York, Oregon, and Vermont. At least ten other states are considering similar measures, and the proposed Bottle Recycling Climate Protection Act, introduced in Congress in 2007, would levy a five-cent deposit on all beverage containers in all states that do not already have a successful deposit program.

• Ten states ban e-waste from landfills and incinerators: California, Connecticut, Maine, Massachusetts, Minnesota, New Hampshire, New Jersey, North Carolina, Oregon, and Rhode Island. E-waste there must be recycled through manufacturer take-back programs or municipal collection sites. Producer responsibility laws are under consideration in fourteen more states in 2008.

What You Should Do About Recycling

The three kinds of waste disposal—dumping, burning, and recycling—have been practiced in all cultures since ancient times. Today recycling is getting more attention than ever as a way to solve global energy and resource depletion problems. There is much you can do to reduce waste now and to prepare yourself for the future as the likelihood of mandatory recycling grows.

Research Local Waste Management Policy

How does your community handle municipal solid waste? Look in the phone book under "Recycling Coordinators" or contact your city or county Department of Sanitation or Department of Public Works to find out how your trash is collected (by private companies or municipal agencies) and where it goes. Officials should be able to estimate total waste produced in your area, how much of that is currently recycled or composted, landfill capacity, and local fees for each kind of disposal.

These agencies can also explain the laws and regulations that determine the content of the waste stream in your area. For example, if you live in a bottle-bill state, curbside recycling bins are less likely to contain returnable beverage containers because residents are more likely to drop off used bottles at redemption centers to get their deposits back, or donate them in school or charitable fund-raising drives away from home. Some cities, such as Seattle, ban paper and cardboard from nonrecyclable waste, with enforcement penalties for apathetic residents who put recyclable material in the garbage can. Seattle and San Francisco are among the first communities to make food scrap recycling mandatory; find out whether you may or must mix food scraps and yard trimmings to be hauled away and composted instead of disposed of in landfills.

Your local solid waste management agency can also tell you when and where e-waste collection events are scheduled, and e-waste recycling organizations such as the Basel Action Network and the Electronics Take-Back Coalition can provide you with lists of manufacturers and local retailers that accept old electronics. Depending on where you live, you may be able to use the U.S. Postal Service's free e-waste recycling program. In 2008, post offices in ten metropolitan areas including Los Angeles, San Diego, Chicago, and Washington, D.C., began providing free envelopes for customers to mail in small electronics such as digital cameras, MP3 players, and inkjet cartridges.

Understand the Debate

What costs your community more—recycling or throwing trash away? The answer to that question is controversial because every method of waste disposal has environmental, economic, and human health benefits and costs that are sometimes hard to measure. The U.S. Environmental Protection Agency has determined that recycling makes good sense because it conserves natural resources, and almost all recycling processes save energy compared to production using virgin materials. But the federal government does not simply mandate recycling because recycling is a local issue.

The structure and success of a recycling program depends on a community's resources, location, the demand for recovered materials, and just how "green" community sentiment is. Practical factors have a significant influence. For example, disposal fees for landfills and incinerators vary across the country, and may be so much lower than the additional fuel and labor costs of sending separate trucks to collect recyclables that a city with a budget crisis has to give up its recycling program, as New York City did in 2002. (It was reinstated in 2004.) West Coast residents are viewed in general as "greener" than people elsewhere in the country, more environmentally conscious and more likely to recycle as a moral duty. The fact is, however, that paper recycling rates are high in West Coast states because demand for recycled paper is very high in China, and West Coast recyclers, near Pacific ports, can ship paper waste to Asia and still make a profit. If demand falls and there is a sudden glut of used paper, as there was with newsprint in the early 1990s, and no one will take it at any price, then much more will be burned or landfilled, no matter how conservation-minded people are.

You'll have a better understanding of the recycling debate if you get information from reliable sources; if comparisons of recycling, incineration, and landfilling present factual evidence, not just opinion; and if you consider the big picture—how waste is produced before it gets to the curbside recycling bin, and what happens to it after the bin is picked up from your house.

Learn the Do's and Don't's of Recycling

Every community has its own guidelines for what should and should not be recycled and how the process should take place. The National Recycling Coalition offers these general tips, whether you presort recyclables or not, whether you put them in curbside bins or drop them at collection centers:

The cleaner and drier recyclable materials are, the easier and cheaper they are to process. Rinse out cans and bottles, remove caps from bottles and plastic jugs, and don't recycle napkins or containers that are contaminated with food. Follow the rules for recycling household hazardous waste, which usually has to be disposed of separately.

Practice Source Reduction

The best way to manage solid waste is to avoid creating it in the first place. Source reduction is waste prevention, which includes reuse. You can practice source reduction at home, school, and in your community by changing your behavior and thinking of the environmental impact of a product before you make a purchase. The Environmental Defense Fund (EDF) offers the following useful advice:

You can avoid the plastic-versus-paper-bag dilemma by getting into the habit of shopping with reusable canvas or string bags. Buy products with as little unnecessary packaging as possible and there will be much less to throw away. Learn to recognize and buy products with recycled content. For example, if the unprinted side of a paper box, such as a cereal box, is gray and not white, it's made from recycled paper. Use both sides of a piece of paper before disposing of it.

Beware of the words "recyclable" and "biodegradable" in product descriptions, which may be designed to boost sales more than address environmental concerns. According to the EDF, "Many materials are technically 'recyclable,' but what matters is what you can recycle in existing local programs. A 'recycled' product or container is actually made from materials that have been used before. . . . Particularly misleading are claims that certain plastic products are 'biodegradable.' The truth is that 'degradable' plastics don't degrade in modern landfills and, at best, merely, break up into smaller pieces. . . . They interfere with plastics recycling and end up creating more problems than they solve."

Try to repair broken items to prolong their life. If you no longer want an item, try to find someone who does before you throw it away. That, too, is recycling.

The editors have compiled the following list of organizations concerned with the issues debated in this book. The descriptions are derived from materials provided by the organizations. All have publications or information available for interested readers. The list was compiled on the date of publication of the present volume; the information provided here may change. Be aware that many organizations take several weeks or longer to respond to inquiries, so allow as much time as possible.

Association of Postconsumer Plastic Recyclers (APR)
2000 L St. NW, Ste. 835, Washington, DC 20006
(202) 316-3046
e-mail: salexander@cmrgroup4.com
Web site: www.plasticsrecycling.org

APR is a national trade association that represents more than eighteen hundred companies that acquire, reprocess, and sell the by-product of more than 90 percent of the post-consumer plastic processing capacity in North America, including independent recycling companies of all sizes, processing numerous resins. APR advocates the recycling of all post-consumer plastic packaging, 95 percent of which is PET (soda and water bottles, medicine containers) or HDPE (milk, water, laundry detergent bottles, and toys), and supports multi-stream (consumer-sorted) curbside collection programs. The APR *Design for Recyclability Guidelines*, available on its Web site, describes numerous ways in which plastic packaging can be designed to increased its recyclability.

Competitive Enterprise Institute (CEI)
1001 Connecticut Ave. NW, Washington, DC 20036
(202) 331-1010 • fax: (202) 331-0640
e-mail: info@cei.org
Web site: http://cei.org

CEI, founded in 1984, is a nonprofit public policy think tank based on unregulated private enterprise and limited government. CEI questions climate change science and the need to reduce oil imports and opposes environmental regulation, including mandatory recycling programs and plastic bag bans. Publications available on its Web site include an updated archive of news articles, issue analyses, congressional testimony, editorials, and other publications such as the 2008 book *Blue Planet in Green Shackles*, the 2007 report *Mandated Recycling of Electronics: A Lose-Lose-Lose Proposition*, and the 2008 articles "The Whole Truth About Plastic Bags" and "Hanging Onto the Trash."

Container Recycling Institute (CRI)
89 East Lake Shore Trail, Glastonbury, CT 06033
(202) 263-0999
e-mail: container-recycling@container-recycling.org
Web sites: www.container-recycling.org • www.bottlebill.org

Founded in 1991, CRI is a nonprofit research and public education organization that studies and promotes alternatives for reducing container and packaging waste and seeks to shift the environmental and social costs of recycling and disposing of container waste from government and taxpayers to producers and consumers. The institute supports and lobbies for federal and state bottle bills (beverage container redemption programs based on a ten-cent deposit per unit). The CRI Web site has abundant student-friendly features, including recycling awareness exercises and classroom projects, a news archive, recycling rate charts and fact sheets, and visuals-loaded downloadable reports such as "Waste and Opportunity: U.S. Beverage Container Recycling Scorecard," the quarterly newsletter *Container and Packaging Recycling Update*, and the *Bottle Bill Resource Guide*.

Earth911.org
14646 N. Kierland Blvd., Ste. 100, Scottsdale, AZ 85254
(480) 889-2650
e-mail submit: http://earth911.org/resources/contact-us
Web site: http://earth911.org

Earth911 is an online project of communications and cause marketing company Global Alerts/Cause Media, designed to deliver nonpartisan, actionable local information about recycling and other environmental issues to consumers. Resources include a 1-800-CLEANUP hotline, videos about waste recycling and disposal, product reviews, local recycling news stories, and a comprehensive directory of some seventy-four thousand U.S. recycling centers.

Electronics TakeBack Coalition
60 29th St., Ste. 230, San Francisco, CA 94110
(415) 206-9595 (CA) or (512) 326-5655 (TX)
e-mail: info@e-takeback.org
Web site: www.computertakeback.com

Originally founded as the Computer TakeBack Campaign, the Electronics TakeBack Coalition is a partnership of environmental and consumer groups, including the Basel Action Network, Environmental Law and Policy Center, Friends of the Earth, GRRN, INFORM, and Silicon Valley Toxics Coalition. The coalition promotes responsible recycling in the electronics industry through so-called green engineering and design principles that extend product life and reduce toxicity; manufacturer voluntary national programs to take back and recycle computers, televisions, cell phones, and other electronics for free when purchasers are through with them; and laws prohibiting hazardous e-waste in U.S. landfills and dumping of e-waste in developing countries. Materials available on the coalition's Web site include PowerPoint presentations, fact sheets, action plans, legislative overviews, and reports such as "Recycling Your Computer: Which Computer Companies Will Take Back Your Old Computer?"

Grassroots Recycling Network (GRRN)
PO Box 282, Cotati, CA 94931
e-mail: Chris Sparnicht at www.grrn.org/contact/index.php?cid=2
Web site: www.grrn.org

GRRN was founded in 1996 on the principle of Zero Waste—maximizing recycling, minimizing waste, reducing consumption and ensuring that products are made to be reused, repaired, or recycled back into nature or the marketplace. The organization devotes detailed sections of its Web site to Campus Zero Waste (recycling and reuse on college campuses) and Kids Recycle! (tools for students and teachers such as poster and recycling campaigns and instructions for composting, vermi-composting, and pollution prevention). GRRN also publishes the monthly e-newsletter *GreenYes*.

INFORM

5 Hanover Square, New York, NY 10004-2638
(212) 361-2400
Web site: www.informinc.org

INFORM was founded in 1973 by Joanna D. Underwood to document the environmental impact of business practices, identify practical improvements, and spread this information to the public. Since Underwood's departure in 2006, the project has refocused its mission on three activities: responsible use and disposal of commercial and residential cleaning products; extended producer responsibility for all stages in a product's life cycle, including funding safe recycling and disposal programs; and INFORM Media, video, and Web products such as *The Secret Life of Cell Phones*. Waste prevention videos, fact sheets, reports, and news archives are available on its Web site.

Institute of Scrap Recycling Industries (ISRI)

1615 L St. NW, Washington, DC 20036-5610
(202) 662-8500 • fax: (202) 626-0900
e-mail: davidkrohne@isri.org
Web site: www.isri.org

ISRI is the national trade association of the recycling and reprocessing industry, including metal, plastics, paper, electronics, glass, textiles, and rubber. Its member companies employ more than fifty thousand people in three thousand facilities, 80 percent of which are in the United States. Resources on its Web site include recycling price statistics and compliance guidelines, news and updates about issues such as metals theft, and schedules of local chapter and national meetings. ISRI publishes the bimonthly magazine *Scrap*.

Keep America Beautiful (KAB)
1010 Washington Blvd., Stamford, CT 06901
(203) 323-8987 • fax: (203) 325-9199
e-mail: info@kab.org
Web site: www.kab.org

KAB is the nation's largest nonprofit public education and community improvement organization whose network of more than 560 city, county, statewide, and international affiliates engages millions of volunteers in programs that prevent litter; reduce, reuse, recycle, and properly manage waste materials, and clean up and beautify their neighborhoods. Educational resources include the kindergarten through grade six classroom curriculum supplement Waste In Place and the six-lesson program Clean Sweep U.S.A., which offers twenty-two Web-based projects that require middle and high school students to examine waste management issues at the national, state, and local levels.

National Recycling Coalition (NRC)
805 15th St. NW, Ste. 425, Washington, DC 20005
e-mail: info@nrc-recycle.org
Web site: www.nrc-recycle.org

The NRC is the largest national nonprofit advocacy group that promotes all aspects of waste reduction, reuse, recycling, and composting in North America. Founded in 1978, the NRC's objective is zero waste and sustainable economies. Among its many public programs, which aim to increase beverage bottle recycling rates, recycling of electronic scrap, and environmentally sound management of natural resources, are America Recycles Day, Reuse-a-Shoe, the annual college competition RecycleMania, and the Coca-Cola/NRC Bin Grant Program. Resources for consumers available on the NRC Web site include links to local recycling agencies, a recycling calculator, and fact sheets such as "Top 10 Items to Recycle."

Natural Resources Defense Council (NRDC)
40 West 20th St., New York, NY 10011
(212) 727-2700 • fax: (212) 727-1773
e-mail: nrdcinfo@nrdc.org
Web site: www.nrdc.org

NRDC, founded in 1970, is a nonprofit environmental action organization of 1.2 million members and a staff of more than three hundred scientists, lawyers, and policy experts. Its mission is the protection of the earth's natural and biological systems. Its main priorities are curbing global warming, reducing America's dependence on oil, saving wildlands, reviving ocean ecosystems, eliminating toxic chemicals in the environment, and speeding the greening of China. The NRDC publishes in-depth articles on recycling issues such as *Trash Landings: How Airlines and Airports Can Clean Up Their Recycling Programs* and *Too Good to Throw Away: Recycling's Proven Record.*

Solid Waste Association of North America (SWANA)
1100 Wayne Ave., Ste. 700, Silver Spring, MD 20910
(800) GO-SWANA • fax: (301) 589-7068
e-mail: info@swana.org
Web site: www.swana.org/www/TECHNICALDIVISIONS/
WasteReductionRecyclingComposting/tabid/111/Default.aspx

SWANA is the professional association of municipal and commercial solid waste management operators in North America. It sponsors the annual WASTECON conference, conducts seminars and training programs, and publishes the bimonthly journal *MSW Management.* Its Web site's technical division Waste Reduction, Recycling & Composting aims to develop best practices that balance environmental sustainability and the budgetary constraints of municipal solid waste disposal agencies.

StopWaste.org
1537 Webster St., Oakland, CA 94612
(510) 891-6500 • fax: (510) 893-2308
Web site: www.stopwaste.org

StopWaste is the free technical assistance service of Alameda County, California, hailed as a model program in coordinating residential and food-scrap recycling efforts, supporting waste prevention, conserving water and energy, and using resources more efficiently. Students and teachers can find information on the Web site about the irecycle@school recycling program, Wonders of a Worm Bin, Where to Find Low-Cost Stuff, Tips for Reducing Waste, and a free 4Rs Teaching Kit.

U.S. Environmental Protection Agency (EPA)
Educational Resources
Ariel Rios Bldg., 1200 Pennsylvania Ave. NW, Washington, DC 20460
(202) 272-0167 • TTY: (202) 272-0165
Web sites: www.epa.gov/students • www.epa.gov/highschool

U.S. Environmental Protection Agency (EPA)
Resource Conservation Challenge
Ariel Rios Bldg., 1200 Pennsylvania Ave. NW, Washington, DC 20460
(202) 272-0167 • (202) 272-0165
- **Educational Resources**
  Web sites: www.epa.gov/students • www.epa.gov/highschool
- **Resource Conservation Challenge**
  Web site: www.epa.gov/epawaste/rcc/index.htm

The EPA is the official source of recycling and waste reduction statistics, pending and in-force legislation, policy recommendations, and educational resources. The three Web sites listed above are focused on material and programs useful to student researchers and consumers. In particular, the Resource Conservation Challenge offers guidelines to achieve a 35 percent national recycling rate by 2008, focusing on paper, food scraps and yard trimmings, and packaging/container materials.

Books

Lori Baird and the Editors of *Yankee Magazine, Don't Throw It Out: Recycle, Renew, and Reuse to Make Things Last.* Emmaus, PA: Rodale, 2007.

Elizabeth Grossman, *High Tech Trash: Digital Devices, Hidden Toxics, and Human Health.* Washington, DC: Shearwater, 2006.

Daniel Imhoff, *Paper or Plastic: Searching for Solutions to an Overpackaged World.* New York: Sierra Club, 2005.

William McDonough and Michael Braungart, *Cradle to Cradle: Remaking the Way We Make Things.* New York: North Point, 2002.

Richard C. Porter, *The Economics of Waste.* Washington, DC: RRF (Resources for the Future), 2002.

Elizabeth Rogers and Thomas M. Kostigen, *The Green Book.* New York: Three Rivers, 2007.

Heather Rogers, *Gone Tomorrow: The Hidden Life of Garbage.* New York: New, 2006.

Mark Roseland, *Toward Sustainable Communities: Resources for Citizens and Their Governments.* Gabriola Island, BC, Canada: New Society, 2005.

Elizabeth Royte, *Garbage Land: On the Secret Trail of Trash.* New York: Back Bay, 2006.

Giles Slade, *Made to Break: Technology and Obsolescence in America.* Cambridge, MA: Harvard University Press, 2006.

Alex Steffen, ed., *Worldchanging: A User's Guide for the 21st Century.* Foreword by Al Gore. New York: Abrams, 2008.

Carol Steinfeld and David Del Porto, *Reusing the Resource: Adventures in Ecological Wastewater Recycling.* Concord, MA: EcoWaters, 2007.

Crissy Trask, *It's Easy Being Green: A Handbook for Earth-Friendly Living*. Layton, UT: Gibbs Smith, 2006.

Carl A. Zimring, *Cash for Your Trash: Scrap Recycling in America*. Piscataway, NJ: Rutgers University Press, 2005.

Periodicals and Internet Sources

Daniel K. Benjamin, "Recycling Rubbish: Eight Great Myths About Waste Disposal," *PERC Policy Series, Issue PS-28*, Property and Environment Research Center, September 2003. www.perc.org/pdf/ps28.pdf.

Computer TakeBack Campaign, "Recycling Your Computer," *Computer TakeBack.com*, August 17, 2007. www.computertakeback.com/docUploads/using_takeback_programsv10.pdf.

Environmental Defense Fund, "Precycling: Shopping for Future Generations," March 7, 2007. www.edf.org/article.cfm?contentid=2194.

Environmental Protection Agency, "Buying Recycled," *Municipal Solid Waste (MSW)*, n.d. www.epa.gov/garbage/buyrec.htm.

Jim Fedako, "Recycling: What a Waste!" *Ludwig von Mises Institute*, September 22, 2005. http://mises.org/story/1911.

Jennifer Gitlitz and Pat Franklin, "Water, Water Everywhere: The Growth of Non-Carbonated Beverages in the United States," *Container Recycling Institute*, February 2007.

Jennifer Hattam, "Talking Trash: Reduce, Reuse, Rejoice," *Sierra*, November/December 2005. www.sierraclub.org/sierra/200511/trl.asp.

Laura E. Huggins, "Get Real on Going 'Green,'" *Washington Times*, April 18, 2008.

Waldemar Ingdahl, "A New Stream of Thought on Recycling: Let Machines, Not People, Sort the Trash," *American*, September 10, 2007.

Olga Kharif, "E-Waste: Whose Problem Is It?" *Business Week*, March 17, 2008.

Brendan I. Koerner, "Paper Recycling—Is It Worth It?" *Slate*, April 29, 2008. www.slate.com/id/2190164.

———, "Thou Shalt Sort Thy Plastics," *Slate*, May 6, 2008. www.slate.com/id/2190734.

Robert Lilienfeld, "It's Time for Us All to Get Involved," *ULS Report*, Use Less Stuff, April-May-June 2008. http://use-less-stuff.com.

Andrew P. Morriss, "Recycling: A Success Story," *PERC Reports*, vol. 22, no. 3, Property and Environment Research Center, September 2004. www.perc.org/articles/article453.php.

Sara Schaefer Munoz, "The Dark Side of 'Green' Bulbs,'" *Wall Street Journal*, January 24, 2008.

National Resources Defense Council, "The Past, Present, and Future of Recycling: Recycling's Up, But So Is Trash," *NRDC Issues: Green Enterprise*, March 28, 2008.

Mary Pfaffko, "The Paper vs. Plastic Conundrum," *Audubon Society of the District of Columbia*, 2007. www.dcaudubon.org/node/6199.

Jamie Reno, "Rising Ripoffs," *Newsweek*, May 19, 2008.

Reusable Bags.com, "Recycling Can Fix This, Right?" n.d. www.reusablebags.com/facts.php?id=5.

Kenneth Stier, "Waste Morphing into 'Resource Transformation' Business," *Green: The Color of Money*, CNBC.com, April 18, 2008. www.cnbc.com/id/24049040.

Jennifer Weeks, "Future of Recycling," *CQ Researcher*, vol. 17, no. 44, December 14, 2007.

INDEX

number of communities
with, 76, *77*
success, 126
PC Recycler, 56
PET plastics, 17, 65, 97, 127
Philadelphia, PA, 8
Phillips, Tom, 22–23
Plastic bags
are better for environment,
103–107, *104*
are not better for
environment, 108–116
lack of biodegradability,
111
litter, 106, 109, *113*
Plastics
biodegradability of, 104, 105,
111, 132
from e-waste, 45
PET, 17, 65, 97, 127
recyclability of, 17, 127
recycling rates, 20, *110*
reusing and recycling, 15,
34–35
See also Bottle bills
Pollution
carbon emissions
from paper, 33, 34
recycling reduces, 12–13
sustainable packaging
reduces, 20
lead, 42, 109
litter, 93, 106, 109, *113*
methane emissions, 15
from paper vs. plastic bags,
105
Polyethylene, 114
Portland, ME, 80
Portland, OR, 111

Presorting. *See* Sorting by
citizens
Producer dematerialization, 55
Producer take-back programs.
See Producer responsibility
Producers. *See* Original
equipment manufacturers
(OEMs)
Product design, 19–20
Puckett, Jim, 40, 42, 43, 44
Pytlar, Theodore, 73

R
RecycleBank, 9
Recycling
benefits environment, 31–38
benefits outweigh costs,
11–21
bottle bills are incentive,
92–97
bottle bills are not incentive,
98–101
costs outweigh benefits, 16,
22–30
described, 125
e-waste is a challenge, 50–58
e-waste is dangerous, 39–49
federal role, 130
history, 15–16
main types, 125–126
mandatory programs are not
effective, 84–91
PAYT increases, 75–83
plastic bags are better than
paper bags, 102–107
plastic bags is difficult, 108–
116
presorting decreases curbside,
59–67

PICTURE CREDITS